HANDBOOK OF
EARLY ADVERTISING ART

HANDBOOK OF EARLY ADVERTISING ART

MAINLY FROM AMERICAN SOURCES

—··•◆•··—

by Clarence P. Hornung

TYPOGRAPHICAL
AND
ORNAMENTAL
VOLUME

THIRD EDITION

Expanded with a new collection
of Initials and Alphabets
Selected by Alexander Nesbitt

DOVER PUBLICATIONS, INC., NEW YORK

Published in Canada by General Publishing Company, Ltd., 30 Lesmill Road, Don Mills, Toronto, Ontario. Published in the United Kingdom by Constable and Company, Ltd., 10 Orange Street, London WC 2.

International Standard Book Number: 0-486-20123-6
Library of Congress Catalog Card Number: 54-9264
Manufactured in the United States of America
Dover Publications, Inc.
180 Varick Street
New York, N. Y. 10014

great bulk of the contents remains American in design and spirit.

The historical development of the decorative initial is a fascinating study, a little knowledge of which can be most illuminating to the typographical craftsman. Mr. Nesbitt has sketched this development in a preface to the section on Alphabets and Decorative Initials and in notes on the plates.

All of the new plates in this third edition were photographed directly from the original sources—type specimen books of the 19th century and earlier.

1956   The Publisher

PREFACE TO SECOND REVISED EDITION

The typographical and ornamental material in this volume is a tenfold expansion over the material that appeared in the first edition. All the material has been rephotographed in order to achieve greater clarity. The section containing type specimens has been greatly expanded and reorganized. New sections on borders, signboards, scrolls, rules and panels, ornaments, and ribbons have been added.

The following specimen catalogues were the main sources for this collection: MacKellar, Smiths and Jordan; *New York Type Foundry Specimen of Printing Types Cast* by John T. White; James Conner's Sons; Blomgren and Co. Some material also came from *Ames Guide to Self Instruction in Practical and Artistic Penmanship* and *Real Pen Work Self-Instructor in Penmanship* published by Knowles and Maxim.

The publisher is deeply indebted to S. Guy Oring for his assistance in preparing this volume.

1953   The Publisher

PREFACE TO THIRD REVISED EDITION

Users of the first and second editions of this work, formerly titled EARLY AMERICAN ADVERTISING ART, have indicated a want for more specimens of decorative initials and for full alphabets. The book has accordingly been enlarged by the addition of fifty-two plates of ornamental alphabets and ten plates of borders. The selection and arrangement of the new material was made by Alexander Nesbitt, author of LETTERING and member of the faculties of New York University and of Cooper Union.

It was found that while early American advertising used decorative letters profusely, few of them were designed in America; they were mostly copied from European designs. In order to provide a representative assortment of such letters and alphabets, it was necessary to draw upon European sources as well as American. The qualification AMERICAN was accordingly dropped from the title of this book, but the

CONTENTS

THE PLATES

The illustrations shown on the following plates have been taken, for the most part, from type specimen books representative of the nineteenth century. A careful inspection of these volumes reveals that the cuts not only appear repeatedly in subsequent issues, but in the pages of several different foundries as well. A listing of these source books will be found in the Appendix, together with notes on the plates.

HUMANITY'S PROCLAMATION

Know all Women by these Presents, That from and after the issuance of this order, every male and female child shall be clad in habiliments sufficient to cover comfortably every portion of its person, any dictum of Fashion to the contrary notwithstanding.

CEMETERY PRESCRIPTION

Naked Knees, Soothing Syrups, Female Regulators Murder of the Innocents

BURIED JEWELS
Oceanic Dredging Company

CONTENTMENT
Industry and Frugality

MEDICAL PREPARATION
Distinctively Preventive and Curative

Native MUSICAL Society

RUINED Cathedral TOWER

CANDIDATE'S BITTER-SWEET
Recuperative Cordial for Baffled Aspirants
Taken before Bedtime
1234567890

COCKTAIL'S TODDY DROPS
Delicious Electioneering
Persuasives Freedom of the Ballot
1234567890

CALUMNY POWDERS
Effectual for Destroying
Rivals Sharp and Caustic
1234567890

LOCOMOTIVE AND MARINE ENGINES
PONDEROUS STRENGTH

COMPANIONS IN MISFORTUNE
CAUGHT TOGETHER

GENUINE INTEGRITY GREETING EXERTION

INTERMIGRATION

BRIGHT MORNING RIDERS

EXPERIENCE

DIAPHANOUS GREENHORN
DOCTOR SLIMJOWL, PHYSIOGNOMISTS
1234567890

LONGSHOREMAN
SNAPSHORT ON MANNERS
1234567890

EXTENSIVENESS
MORMON CONTINENCE
1234567890

ROOMINESS
PUSHING ONWARD
12345678

DINNERLESS CIRCUMSTANCES
Craving Appetite
Mournful Reflection and Stomach Dejection
Empty Purse and Empty Larder
1234567890

NATIONAL BANQUET
Spread-Eagleism
After-Dinner Patriotic Platitudes
1234567890

FRUGAL REPAST
Crunching Dry Luncheon
1234567890

QUIET MEAL
Washing-Day Dinner
12345678

VERISIMILITUDE
Frostie Wynde, Cheek Painter
Red Nose, Numb Toes
12345678

HABITATION
Building Associations
12345678

SPOUTS, PLUMBER
Eaves-Dropping and Pocket Leaks Stopped
1234567890

EOLIAN SOUNDS
Mosquito's Baritone Minstrelsy

NIGHT VOICES
Screechowl and Nighthawk

PROMPTNESS
Dunner and Bummer

MODERNIZED
Commonwealth Insurance
123456

UNSELFISH
American Statesmen
123456

MORTGAGE
Foreclosure Notice
123456

BUNCOMB
State 23 House

ENTERTAINMENTS
Patience Handie, Children's Seamstress
123456

PERPENDICULARITY
Prof. Petroleum's Pyrotechnics
1234567890

ETHIOPIAN Darkness
123456

INDIAN Mounds

BATMOUSEM'S ANTIQUITIES

Owlet's Review

HONOURED MEMORIALS

Scissors Chronicle

Quillpen's OPINION Platform

HUGE Prairie BISON

CIRCUMAMBULATION

COMMENDATION

FOR SALE AT AUCTION BY.

DEMACOT

tomemen

RAIL-ROAD.

Steam Ships.

TIME

hares

MAINE

$12345

MIRS

$1640

GUN

haul

RIE

note
ME
TE

CONTENTMENT ASSURANCE CORPORATION
Benny Volence, Heart Doctor
The heart of Hope with Care shall cope, and pitch it down
Oblivion's poppied slope.
1234567890

POORMAN'S ACCOMMODATION COMPANY
Hornpipe & Pirouette, Wheelwrights
Unhallowed gold rankly smells in churchyard mould:
A story old, and vainly told.
1234567890

Elegance of True Simplicity, Real Beauty of Contentment
OLDEN CUSTOMS AND HABITS

Lighting a Candle to Discover One's
UNAFFECTEDNESS

STRANGE SECRETS WORTH KNOWING
Persevering Industry the Foundation of Success
Little Savings, Great Gains
1234567890

AURIFEROUS BLACKHILLS
Violent Paroxysmal Attacks of Gold-Fever
Uncle Sam, Medical Doctor

RAILWAY NOTICE
Heavy Men Double Passengers

MODERN AQUATIC
Boytonism Useful for Dodging Troublesome

BLACK THUNDER CLOUDS
Hastening over the Mountain-Ranges

UNCONQUERABLENESS
The Bank of Love and Gentle Humanities

UNDAUNTEDNESS
Gentlefolk's Honourable Company

FRIENDLINESS
Melocotonean Consociation

SHORTNESS
Harmonious Brothers

HORNED
Heroic Mother

HARD-DRINKING BAR-TENDING LADIES
FEMININE CLUBROOMS AND SAMPLING SALOONS
1234567890

MALE CHINESE BRIDGETS
RULE THE ROAST AND TURN THE TOAST
1234567890

ASSOCIATION OF SHEBEARS AND UNSEXED HUMANS MODESTY
UNMITIGATED HUMBUG, PROPRIETY SHAM, DECENCY OBSOLETE

FEMININE CLINIC OPERATIONS HOSPITAL
SURGERY BEFORE FIRESIDE DRUDGERY

HEAVEN'S BLESSING
HOME-CONTENTED WOMANKIND

FASHIONABLE MANUAL
Directions for Respectable Sponging
Indispensable to Diners-Out

IMPERIAL BULLETIN
Eugenie Imperatrice Sneezed
No Unhappy Results

TELEGRAPHIC
Hon. Snooks took an Airing

NIGHT SONGS
Mosquito's Minstrels

COMPOUND EXTRACT
Double Teeth Drawn by Dr. Twistemout

CRABBEDNESS
Bachelors' Characteristic

CRISPINIAN CORNCRUSHERS

PUNCHER'S EYESPARKER

DANCUPID, HYMENIST

SHEARED EQUINES

MUSHMUDDLER

COMMANDER

OCCIDENTAL PRODUCTION

PRUNING SHEARS

MERE HEAD!

the far sound

HINTONE

memento

DNH

MONT

CANTO!

NEW-YORK!

MANUFACTURE

an improvement

PRINTING

MILLINERY RECONSTRUCTION
Obedience and Allegiance
Opening of Milliners' Drawers and Husbands' Purses
Imperative Order from the Congress of Fashion

BUREAU OF MATRIMONY
Cheap for Cash
Brainless, Glib, and Moneyed Husbands
Dressy, High-Notioned Wives

CURRENCY AND FASHION
EXPANSION VERSUS CONTRACTION
1234567890

DEVOURING LOCUSTS
FIVEPERCENT TAX-GATHERERS
1234567890

GOLD SPECULATING BEARS

COALMINE OPENINGS

GRADGRIND'S HOMILETICS

HARDSHELL THEOLOGY

BROAD SCHEMES   SOLID STOCK

HONORABLE BUMMERS

MANNERS

NEARING DANGER
QUICKSAND AND QUAGMIRE

SHREWD MINERS

FRINGED BORDER

SPRINGTIME

ELEGANT PRODUCTS
Foreign and Domestic Invention

CONFUSION
International Gatherings

EMINENT
Defeated Statesmen

MIDSUMMER DREAMINGS

NIMBIFEROUS

MEDIEVAL WATCHTOWER
VAULTED MARBLE

ADVANCE RETREAT
CONQUERED

MORNIN GAZETTE

DIAMOND

ANCIENT WRITINGS
Autobiography of Nebuchodonosor
Handsomely Embossed

EARLY RECORDS
Difficulties of Egyptian Architecture

ENORMOUS
Aquatic Deinotherium

MARRIAGE CERTIFICATES, BAPTISMAL RECORDS
FIRST MORTGAGE BONDS

PUNCHEON'S MUNCHING LUNCHEON
STOMACH FENDERS

TODDISWEET'S LIPDROPS

IMPORTANT PERSONAGE
Boasting Mediocrity Invested with Authority

SPACIOUS VAULTAGE
Tunneled Passages Through Mountains

CIRCUMSCRIBED
Happiness amidst Tribulation

WINSOME
Handsome Babyhood

WAYSIDE
Earning Capacity

PATRIARCH
Honoured Grandam

DEMURE
Smiling Modesty

SUNSET COCKSCROWING
1234567890

BOLDEYED SPOONIES
1234567890

HOOSIER DIVORCES
1234567890

MAIDEN BLUSHES
1234567890

HERMAPHRODITE
1234567890

PANTAMORPHIC
1234567890

FREELOVING AFFINITIES
1234567890

SPLITTING THE DIFFERENCE
Levying Half-and-Half on Producers and
Consumers Middlemen's Exchange

BIGGEST BORES ABOUT
Gimlet-Holes through Cenis and Hoosac

OBJECTS OF INTEREST
Moneys on Deposit in
Saving Banks

GOLDEN-STATE CONTINGENCIES
CHOPSTICK & SCALPLOCK, PACIFIC AGITATORS
1234567890

EDITOR'S PROOFSHEETS
TRIPHAMMER ON FIRST IMPRESSIONS
1234567890

MEDITATIONS ON HEMP SWITCHES
1234567890

SENATORIAL COMPLIMENTS
1234567890

LONGTONGUE DEBATER
1234567890

COURTED PETTICOATS
1234567890

ROUND SHOULDERED PUNCHERS
1234567890

ECONOMICAL CONGRESSMEN

HONEST STATESMANSHIP

MILITARY DILETTANTI

CORN-HUSKING SCENE

BACHELOR FRIEND

RECENT ROGUERY

OCEAN VISION

INSTRUCTORS

STRONGMIND DAUGHTERS

BUNDLE OF BLESSINGS

MAGNETIC INFLUENCE

KITCHEN SONGSTER

STONE ORNAMENT

GARDEN TRUCK

INTERCESSION

SIMMERING

UNQUESTIONABLE PROPOSITIONS

Ornamented Type, like bonbons and gingerbread, may occasionally serve a good purpose; but a neat and elegant PLAIN LETTER is always as welcome and serviceable as bread and butter. This is a self-evident proposition to all who are gifted with that admirable felicity of taste which discovers beauty in simplicity.

Thrifty Housekeeper!   Bountiful Providers!

1234567890

ADMIRABLE OPPORTUNITY

HOUSE TO LET, with all the modern conveniences, except water-closet, gas and bath, to a nice, genteel family without any children.   Fine pigsty and dog-kennel in the yard.

Splendid Residence!   Inviting Accessories!

1234567890

PUNCHMUG'S GYMNASIUM
MILLING MACHINES
Polite Antics, Monkey Capers,
Fancy Accomplishments
Principal Rooms, 389 Fisticuff Street
Delightsome Recreations!

DISTINGUISHED KEYSTONEMEN
1234567890

NATURE'S CROCHET GRANARY
1234567890

COURTEOUS GENTLEMEN
1234567890

EXCELLING ADORNMENT
123456789

WOMANLY ELEGANCE
12345678

DISINTERESTED BENEVOLENCE

Mr. Judas Hypocrite, a retired scoundrel in good health, will send free to all applicants a sure recipe for all human maladies.   No attention given unless ten stamps be sent.

Delicate and Refined Roguery.

GRATUITOUS EXHIBITION.

Daily, on the Portico of Universe Hotel, a fine assortment of Fashionable Young Dandies, with Eyeglasses, Cigars, Moustaches, and Impudence.

Ladies' Especial Delectation.

GOUGEM GRAB BANK.

Capital secured in the Directors' Pockets. Ten per cent. Premium.

Depositors fully paid in promises.

BEAUSNARES
Ornamented Flowers.
Mrs. Eve, Inventor.

Quosque tandem abutere, Catili
na, patientia nostra? quamdiu nos
etiam furor este tuus eludet? qu
em ad finem sese effrenata jacta

ABCDEFGHIJKLMNOPQR

$ 1234567890

THE GLOBE.

GENEVA GAZETTE.

THE SYRACUSE JOURNAL.

MORNING CONCERT

Signora Earsplitto's 892d Farewell Concert.   She will sing with pathos "My heart is sad! my pocket lean!" *Lachrymose Circumstance!*

PREMIUM

Immediate Duck-Hatcher! Patent Secured 123456

REFLECTOR

Fireside Companion 123456

PROGRESSED
OBSERVER

SIDELONG GLANCES
Bashful Maidenhood's Chances
1234567890

REAPERS
Straddling Creepers

CRICKETERS
Gothamitic Chronicler

AMERICA
Union Guardian

EXTRA
Constitution

HOUSEHOLD BENEDICTION
Grandmother Busy Knitting and Rocking
Skein-Entangling Kitten
1234567890

PEACEFUL SUNSET
Spectacled Grandfather's Slumbers
12345678

SADNESS KILLERS
Childhood's Frolicking Humours
12345678

HEART-GRIPS
Maiden's Gentle Manners
1234567

MORNING HERALD.

PENNSYLVANIA.

MADISONIAN.

SHOREAN

PLUMBS

NUTRITIOUS ALIMENT FOR NOTIONALS
Gathered from Macadamized Roads, Philosoph's Prepared Granitic Breadstuff
Superior to the Finest Sawdust Flour
1234567890

LIEMONGER'S LABORATORY
State Secrets and Cabinet Plans Manufactured to Order
1234567890

SHORTCOMMONS UNIVERSITY
Conducted on Approved Grahamitic Principles
1234567890

EVENING'S LENGTHENING SHADOWS
Exercises in Attenuation for Persons of Inordinate Obesity

GRENADIERS IN SOLID PHALANX
Marching to the Front on the Extra Double Quick

POPPIED DRAUGHT
Screaming Babies' Final Quieter
1234567890

PUBLIC VENDUE
Jack Fibalittle, Auctioneer
12345678

IMPORTANT!
Fuglemen, Attention!
12345678

SIMPLE ELEGANCE BETOKENETH HIGH CULTIVATION
COMB & BRUSH, SQUATTER EJECTORS
1234567890

SUMPTUOUS DISTRIBUTION OF PRODUCTS
ORCHARDS REPLENISHED
1234567890

NARROWMIND ON SELF-CHEATING
1234567890

ICHTHYOLOGICAL POLLYWOGISMS
1234567890

ASSINEGO SCIENTIFIC PRINCIPLES
1234567890

MYRMIDONS OF BACHELORS
1234567890

RUMINANTIA'S REFLECTIONS ON CUD-CHEWING
1234567890

INCOMPRESSIBLE MEGALOSAURIANS

MULTITUDINOUS MONOSYLLABLES

UNBEDIZENED FEMININITIES

DANDIES' CONDENSED ESSENCE

COMPRESSED·STERNUM

CIRCUMSCRIBED CIRCUMSTANCES

ASTOUNDING VELOCIPEDIC EPIDEMIC

GIGANTIC SCHEMERS

BEAUTIFUL MAIDEN, FAIRER THAN MORN
WHIFF & SNIFF, TOBACCONISTS
1234567890

BENIGNITY AND DIGNITY IN UNITY
1234567890

MATUTINAL MELODIOUS NOTES
1234567890

INTELLECTUAL LEANNESS
1234567890

PHRENOLOGUS BUMTIBUS
1234567890

SENSIBLE PLAINNESS
1234567890

MODERN LIBERALISM
Reasons Why
My Opinions should Govern Yours

LANDGRABBING
Railways Built without Means
Nursed by Congress

MOIETY BORERS' SALVAGE
Dangerous Wrecks Ashore Destroying the
Ship of State

INSTANT REPEAL
Demanded by the Potential People!

Quosque tandem abutere, Ca talina, patientia nostra? qua mdiu nos etiam furor iste tu us eludet? quem ad finem se se effrenata jactabit audacia?

ABCDEFGHIJKLMNOP

*Quousque tandem abu-
tere, Catilina, patientia
nostra? quamdiu nos
etiam furor iste tuus el*

ABCDEFGHIJKLM

New York, Ohio.

Massachusetts.

ABCDEFGHIJK

Quousque tandem abutere,
Catilina, patientia nostra?
quamdiu nos etiam furor is

ABCDEFGHIJKLMNOP
$ 1234567890 £

EXPANDING CHILDHOOD
Modest Broad Belles
Smotherbrain, Juvenile Taskmaster
1 2 3 4 5 6

ROTUND INFANT
Fast Ponies
Infallible Yeast Powder
1 2 3 4 5 6

EXHIBITION!
Fat Girl!
Mammoth Squashes
1 2 3 4 5 6

BOBOLINKUM
Merriest Summer Whistler
1234567

BLUEBIRDS
Feathery Pioneers
123456

TURRET
Watch-Towers
1234

AMANER
OLDER!
HORN
HER
LON

MERITS

munster.

MAINE

miltons.

MORE

Meid
ran
ha

ME

BEN

SALT NOTICE
None matin
BREWINGTON 184
Herman Fitchclas
HONECLIFT
animated

Corning, Dunkirk, MASSACHUSETTS.

THERNTON

VICTORY

PEREN

FORHAR

indomin

CHORIN

hounds

DERMINA
EHd
roe

SLENDERSHANKED

PERPENDICULAR
Broomstick's Feminine Defenders

COMPRESSION
Monolithic Monument

UPSHOOTING
Mountain Formation

MULTITUDINOUS MONOPOLIES
LOCOMOTION BY PERSONAL PEDANEOUS EFFORTS
1234567890

MUTUAL FRIENDS
BROTHERHOOD OF POLITICIANS
1234567890

BRIGANTINES
TREASURE FREIGHTED
1234567890

Quousque tandem abutere, Catili na, patientia nostra? quamdiu no etiam furor iste tuus eludet? que ad finem sese effrenata jactabit audacia? nihilne te nocturnum præsidium palatii nihil urbis vi

ABCDEFGHIJKLMNOPQR
STUVWXYZÆŒ

Quousque tandem a butere, Catilina patientia nostra? qua

ABCDEFGHIJKL AKMNVWY

Declaration

WYNDHAM

HOBFIELD

Washington.

Harmonist

BCDEFG

Y.W.MAN

HUDSON

Stateman

IMMENSE

Great Boulder-Stone

Bending Bough

NIMBLE Rock

Land-Slide

BROAD hits

Hill-Side

GRIM Dwarf

Anarboy

MAYNE.

Salsbury

MAIN

monitor

BALSAM OF SUNSHINE
Heaven's Benefaction
Dropt on Ocean's Tide and Mountain's Side

GASEOUS LOZENGES
Sugar-Coated
Giddy Swells and Flirting Belles

UNIVERSAL HOUSE-CLEANER
Sure and Pure
Combination of Strong Arms, Brooms, and Brushes

INCREDIBLE EXHIBIT
Fireside Grumbler

Caught while Snapping
at his Wife

REMARKABLE!

Economical Housekeeping

EXTRACT OF LAUGHTER
For Fireside Use
Exhilarating Draught for Heavy Hearts

HYDRATE OF CHLORAL
Gentle Quiet
Balm of Peace to Nervous Spirits

PNEUMATIC TUNNEL
Thousands Blown Through every Minute

CHATTERING GIRLHOOD
Delicious Nothings and Musical Nonsense

BRAIN-DEFENDERS

Tender Gender's Hempen Fenders

SNEAKSOUL & HITBEHIND
Underhand Operators and Professors of Trickery

RINGNOSED TAXPAYERS
Independent Suffrage, Absurd Hypothesis

TRADE SECRETS
Business Drummers' Directory

PERFORATING ENGINES
Inquisitive Neighbours, Seaside Mosquitos

BUILDING COMMISSION

Man of the Mountain

astride the People

BUDDING BLOSSOMS

Grandpa's Sweet Darling and Grandma's Most Precious
Otherfolk's Smothered Abomination

ECONOMICS OF AGRICULTURE
Amateur Growing of Beets, Turnips, and Cabbages
Cheap at a Dollar Apiece

FASHIONABLE ACADEMIES
Learning Homœopathically Administered in Driblets
Liberal Charges, Awful Extras

CONCERT SALOONS
Airline Lightning Railway to Devildom
Most Direct Route

MORTGAGES
Modern Homestead Improvement
Equal to French Roofs

ESQUIRE OFFICEHOLDER'S INTRODUCTORY

Mysteries of Bill-Sticking

The Superlative Art of Sticking your Friends and Creditors Practically Considered

Sticking to Truth a Lost Accomplishment

1234567890

PROFESSOR LIGHTFINGER ON WAYS AND MEANS

Questionable Arrangements

Purchasing Public Supplies from Yourself and Approving your own Bills

Public Means Utilized in Private Ways

1234567890

METHODS OF EXAMINING WITNESSES

Customary Practices

Truth Drawn out in Driblets, Honest Testifiers Confounded

Confining Witnesses to the Question

1234567890

ANCIENT BARBARIC AMUSEMENTS

For Royalty and the Rabble

Gladiatorial Contests and Encounters with Wild Beasts

Tournaments, Bull Baiting, Boar Hunting

1234567890

MODERN ENTERTAINMENTS

Barnumian Charioteering

Trapeze Daredevilism, Pugilistic Ruffianism

Shortgowned Theatricals

1234567890

SWERVING FROM STRAIGHT LINES
Writing Another Man's Name
Borrowing Securities, Raising Certificates, Cornering Breadstuffs
Sinuous Tracks of Brandied Pedestrians
1234567890

CELESTIAL RESERVOIRS EXHAUSTED
Absorbed by Coggia's Comet

Replenishment by Atmospheric

Water-Pumps from Cloudland

Commencement of the Reign of Aquarius
1234567890

WESTWARD ON EMPIRE'S TRACK
Primeval Innocence and Bliss
Fig-Leaf Humanity free from Dilettanti Contaminations of Effete Civilization
Plentiful Absence of Salt, Cigars, Matches and Soap
1234567890

RETURN TO THE HEARTHSTONE
Privations, Dangers, Sickness, Fatigue and Impositions Ended
Contentment and Blissful Repose
1234567890

MIDNIGHT THINKINGS
Pictures of Delight Looming up in Memory
Dismal Swamps and Everglades
1234567890

NATURE'S FORCES UTILIZED
Steam-Power Superseded
Hurricanes and Cyclones Caught and Harnessed
Clouds and Rain on Demand
Complete Subjugation of the Elements
1234567890

HOUSEHOLD ECONOMY
Home Comforts
Heat from Africa, Cold from the North
Bottled for Emergencies
1234567890

HUNDRED-TORNADO WIND-POWER
Oratorical, Musical, Mercantile, Advertising,
Zephyrs for Curtain Lecturers

SCIENTIFIC AGRICULTURE
Harvest Hastened
Postponed at Pleasure

SPANGLE, BEDIZEN AND GARNISH
DEALERS IN GEWGAWS
BEDECKMENTS FOR SUMMER RESORT VISITORS
PECUNIOUS PEOPLE EMBLAZONED
1234567890

BOMBASTIC CHARLATANS
PANTOMIMISTS
PRETENTIOUS DAMES AND DAMSELS
DRESSED FOR PROMENADE
1234567890

ARTISTIC TORQUES
MAGNIFICENT CARCANETS
GOLDEN ORNAMENTS

HANDSOME
ORIENTAL RUBIES

ENORMOUS
AMERICAN DIAMONDS

REPRODUCED
BOHEMIAN GARNITURE

ARABESQUES

URBANE MANNER

HONEST DEALING

GOVERNMENTAL
Contracts for Altering Climates

GRAPHIC CURRENT SKETCHES
Tight Papers
Overdue Promissory Notes, Slim Bank Balances
Unpleasantly Embarrassing
1234567890

SALAD FOR THE FLESHY
Turnip Sprouts
Infallible Regimen for Corpulent Persons
1234567890

REQUISITE OFFICIAL ADJUNCTS
Unblushing Brassiness
Sniffletongue Gobetweens and Persistent Buttonholers
1234567890

SLENDER-WAISTEDNESS
Corseted Divinities with Waspish Affinities
Worrying, Flurrying

CENSUS TAKERS
Youthful Patriarchs,
Youngish Old Women Human Polls
and Chattels

PERQUISITES
Certain Legalized Stealings

RUNABOUT CLACKING MESDAMES
Pannier Humps and Hempen Clumps and Peak-Heeled Stumps
Grouty Husbands' Doleful Dumps

INSIDIOUS POCKET PICKERS
Whisky-Nips, Billiard-Sticks, Jamaica-Flips
Seducing Blondes

GREAT EXTENSION
Stock Script
Broad Plans, Profuse Waterings
Grand Speculation

ELASTIC CURRENCY
Facilities Granted to the Public for Pocket Filling
Everyone his own Note-Stretcher

BUSINESS EXTENDER
Calculated to Overspan the Universal Creation
State Rights Secured

STRONG PRESSURE
Professional Lobbyism Checkmated
Money's Measure

BROADBOTTOMS
Swamps and Cranberry
Patches Sauce for the Goose

QUEER CIRCLES
Eager Purse-Filling
Rings Insatiate Grabbers

Convention of Wiseacres
Representatives of the Statesmanship of Creation

Library of Brain Wonders
Unwritten Books, Unreadable Manuscripts

Equanimous Law-Makers and Riotous Statute-Breakers

Crotchety Obfuscators Plotting with Lackhead Calculators

Magnificent Land Enterprise in Lunaville
Rousing Opportunity

Grandly Terrific Panorama of the Sun!
Admission One Cipher

Contented Home Associations

Racing over the Lawn

Mirthful, Frolicksome, Innocent

Spring's Delightful Morning

Typographic Advertiser

Cheatandlie's Receipts for Fortune-Making

Quillstumper, Government Counsellor

Miss Witsting's Bosom-Cutters

Meddleman's Scandal Sauce

Paternal Stern Rejection, Suitor's Deep Dejection
Double-Quick Oblique Marching

Runaway Couple's Passionate Honeymoon
Half Rations and Hasty Marches

Charging Tender Mamma's Heart
Advancing Infantry

Securing Products of Industry
Raiding on the Public

Overflowing Pockets, Groaning Cellars, Softwool Raiment
Suggestions of Benevolence

Noble-Hearted Men Encased in Virtue's Armour
Awaking to the Reveille

Patiently Waiting Angelic Beckonings
Homeward Marching

Tilthammer & Krowbar, Ironmongers, Ramrod Street
1234567890

Mind's Maga for the Musing Million
1234567890

Crudities on Biped Diversities

Geological Investigations

Presidential Snubbers

Defiance Manual

Roudie's Development of Character

Fuddlers of Conscience

Freedom's Benison

The Grand Exhibition of the Luna-Spiritualistic Association
Common Sense a Disqualification to Membership
Free Admission for Legislators

The Renowned and Honourable Society of Antiquaries
Batwing Hall, Mousing Place, Fossilville

The Capping Stone of Elegant Adornment
Modern Typography

Nature's Incomparable Handiwork
Skilful Artist-Craft

John Bull's Essays on Neutrality

Hellenic Grace Barbaric Strength

Frolicksome Maidenhood Fair as Young Morning

Mirth's Delicious Morsels

Postman and Recorder

Day-Star

Mouser's Curiosities of Exploration
The Old Round Tower of the Norsemen at Newport
Don Quixotte on Windmills

Venerable Obscurity
Black Letter Books hid in Dim Cloisters
Eclipsed Lamps of Knowledge

In Sacred Memory of the Favoured Early Blest
Hallowed Memento

A B C D E F G H I K
L M N O P Q R S T U
V W X Y Z &

a b c d e f g h i j k l m n o p q r s t u v
w x 1 2 3 4 5 6 7 8 9 0 y z

Crumbling Holds of Chivalry
Blackened Mossgrown Fragment of Barbaric Ages
Prison=Houses of Oppression

Sardanapalus's Nightcap
Calfparchment's Archaiological Researches
Toothpick of Apicius

Gropings in Midnight
A Darkness as of Erebus Surrounding
Middle Ages Pictured

Pedagogue's Delectation
Schoolboy's Copybook Pride
Mistress's Delight

Department of our Affairs

Models made to Order

Writ of No-Go

Scire Facias

Morning

Courier

Healthful Sanitary Engineering
Scientific Research
Developing Appliances to abate Contagion
Sure Guarantee of Longevity
1234567890

Latest Telegraphic Despatches
Great Victories
National Horses Win the Imperial Stakes
Patriotic Spirit Aroused
1234567890

Association of Idiosyncrasies
Questions on the Variability of Streaked Lightning
Discussion Every Moonlight Evening
1234567890

Time-Honored Customs
Repealed by Legislative Injunctions
1234567890

Public Speakers
Unterrified Press Opinions
1234567890

Rules for Getting Through the World
Polite Behaviour, Considerate Speech, Deliberate Judgment
Good Breeding is Founded on Good Feeling

Tonics for the Speculative Mind
Adversities are Oftentimes the Bridges of Fortune
Lessons in the School of Experience

Eating Stale Dinners
Waiting for Crumbs from Death's Table

Extravagant Housekeeping
Subsisting upon the Bread of Idleness

Finger-Boards for Life Travellers

Self-Advancement Charity

Mankind's Contentions Develop Inventions

Kind Thoughts and Good Actions

Quaker Philosopher's Stone
Plain Apparel
Changing Fashion-Fancies Disregarded
Richest Silk and Broadcloth
1234567890

Bachelor Warriors
Defeated in Parlour Battles
Sighing Victims
1234567890

Current Baseball Revolution
Business Neglected and Pleasure Projected
Loafers' Paradise

Cheerful Blooming Maiden Singing to the Spinning of the Wheel
Spinning-Wheel and Knitting-Needles

Napoleon Bonaparte Mugginsdorf   Miss Miggie Piggie Dumps

Youngsters' Christmas Savings

Adventurous Chimney Corner Explorings

Constant Trains and Stations at Dram Shops   Messages from Pole to Pole with Despatch
Popular Line to Poor Harbour   Equatorial Telegraph Company

Spending Money before Earning   Sweethearts & Tendersighs

Grand Consolidated Loan Company

Mannitunk Wife Insurance Company

Mathematical Combination Accountant

Lameduck Collections

Wildcat Accommodations

Museum of the Beautiful

Mademoiselle Dilettante's Fashionable Sociables

Crutches to Halters, Balsam to the Wounded

Beauty Triumphant over Strength

Excessive Taxation Brother-Kin to Tyranny and Corruption

Mountebanks Bedecked in Heaven's Livery

Rambles of a Bachelor Seeking his Helpmeet
1234567890

Woman's Smile the Reward of Toil
1234567890

Sympathetic Bosom of Loving Wifehood

Immortality's Entrance Portal

Peacefully Resting

Biblum Pauperum

Corruption's Harvest-Home
Wine & Women

Academy of Humbugs
Endowment

Moneyville Banking Company

Hobby Horses and Spinning Jennies
Society for the Prevention of Cruelty to Babykind
Admirable Institution
1234567890

Lickspittle, Business Borer
Blarney Snares for Green Customers
1234567890

Upwakings of Olden Memories
Sleeping Centuries

Collegiate Boat Racing
Short Strokes

First National Bull=Baiting Arena

Ear-Splitting Monsters
Melodious Night-Screeching Matinée
1234567890

Base=Ball Players
Pitching and Catching on the Fly
1234567890

Freedom's Resting Place
Hail, Columbia

National Centennial
Fairmount

Politician's Vocabulary
Emphatic Damaging Expletives

Dictionary of Slang
Pseudo Gentlemen Editors

Manual of Politeness
Elegantly Illustrated by Old Professors

Graceful and Refined Demeanour
Mountebank Company

Mrs. Simper's Reception
Ninnie Cottage

Quinsigamond Manufacturing Company
Belles-Lettres Professors

United States Senate Chamber
Sniveller, Nosologist

Magnificent Combination
Pacific Railroad

Gentleman Merriwit, Crackajoke Square
Lightfooted Maidenhood

Conclave of the Self-Conceited
Honourable Guild of Ancient Mule Drivers
Skylark on Early Rising
1234567890

Pestiferous Social Malevolents   Conquering Ballroom Heroes

Rosebud and Muslin, Bride Decorators

Bright Variegated Leaves
Delightful Indian Summer Landscape
Mature Womanhood

Delightful Home Memories
Grandma's Golden-Wedding Festival
Auld Lang Syne

Miss Araminta for Inspection this Evening
Angleville, Marble Terrace
Exclusive Privilege of Wealthy Gentlemen Without Entanglements
Opera-Glasses for the Bashful

Benedict's Farewell Meeting with Bachelor Friends
Miriam Butterfly Fenceleaper à Cheval every Brisk Sunny Morning
Moonlight Meeting, Cheerful Greeting

Beautiful Morning in the Lover's Paradise
Trip to the Vale of Falling Waters by the Newly-Wedded
Delightful Summer Excursion

Magnificent Trousseau
Miss Eleonora Goldington's Bridal Presents
Bewildering Wonderment

Aurora Caught Napping
Weekly Meeting of Somnific League
Moonlight Jaunts to Dreamland
1234567890

Uppercrust Residences
Skyward Mansard Domiciles
Outdoor Balloon Elevators
1234567890

Honourary Degree

Illustrated Lectures

United Dairymaids

1234567890

Academy of Science
Propagation of Good Manners
Membership Unlimited
1234567890

Humane Society
Life-Saving Apparatus
12345678

Illuminated Manuscript

National Bank of Metallic

Foundation

1234567890

Benefactors' Pantheon
Asylum for Equines and Canines
Pussy's Fireside Corner
1234567890

Goldlace Regiment
Ostentatious Pomposity
1234567890

Christmas Festivities
Convention of Demented Scientists
1234567890

Weibliche Lehr= und Erziehungs=Anstalten
Stereotypen=Gießerei

Amerikanische National-Literatur
Artistische Zeitung

Das Buch der Natur liegt seit Jahrtausenden aufgeschlagen vor dem Blicke des Menschen

Erfindung der Buchdruckerkunst

Eisenbahn-Maschinenbau

Gesellschaft für Künstler

Humanitäts-Verein

Bibliographisches Institut

Pianofortemagazin und Musikalienhandlung

Bank of Frugaltown
Twenty-Second Mortgage Bonds
1234567890

Sombrous Mist
Life Insurance Company
12345678

Beautiful Trappings
Femininities

Old Limburger
Fragrant

S Wassail Tankard R

Unique Sewing-Machine
To Mend Fractured Reputations
1234567890

Short Folks
Accommodation Bank
12345678

Livefast's Swift Line to Ruination
Without Detention

Portrait Galleries

Sonnenschein nach dem Regen
Tropfstein-Gebilde

Große Freundlichkeit   Der Blumengarten

Licht im Dunkeln   Das Mondlicht

Die Unabhängigkeits-Erklärung
Revolutions-Krieg

Trauer-Weiden

Ancient Scandinavian Mythological Fables   Cloister-buried Manuscripts

Sacred Apostolic Precepts

FROM CLOISTERED CELLS   VALIANT KNIGHTS
GLORIA IN EXCELSIS   MALTA ISLE

Electrical Lamplighters   Perpetual Currency

Molten Silver's Resplendence   Rare Fancy Letter

Arbours Delightsome

Philadelphia yclept by William Penn

L. Johnson & Co.'s Ancient Founderie

Boyhood's Downiness

Primitive Stern and Rugged Virtues   The Brooding Mousing Owl

Ancient Worth Memorials

ABCDEFGHIKLMN

OPQRSTVWXYZ

abcdefghijklmnopqrstu

vwxyz.&1234567890.

ABCDEFGHIJKLMN

OPQRSTUVWXYZ&

Crusader Defender

Public Trump

Mound City

Post

Metropolis

North Star

Union of the States

Nevada Beacon

United States

Union of the States

Nevada Beacon

United States

Union of the States

Nevada Beacon

United States

Union of the States

Nevada Beacon

United States

A B C D E F G H I J K L M N O
P Q R S T U V W X Y Z

a b c d e f g h i j k l m n o p q r s t u v w

x y z &

A B C D E
F G H I J K
L M N O P Q R
S T U V W X Y Z

A A B C D E F G H I J K L M
M N O P Q R S T U V W X Y Z

Whole Arm Capitals may be used for Superscriptions
Ledger Headings and Professional Penmanship where
license and display are permissible, if not desirable.

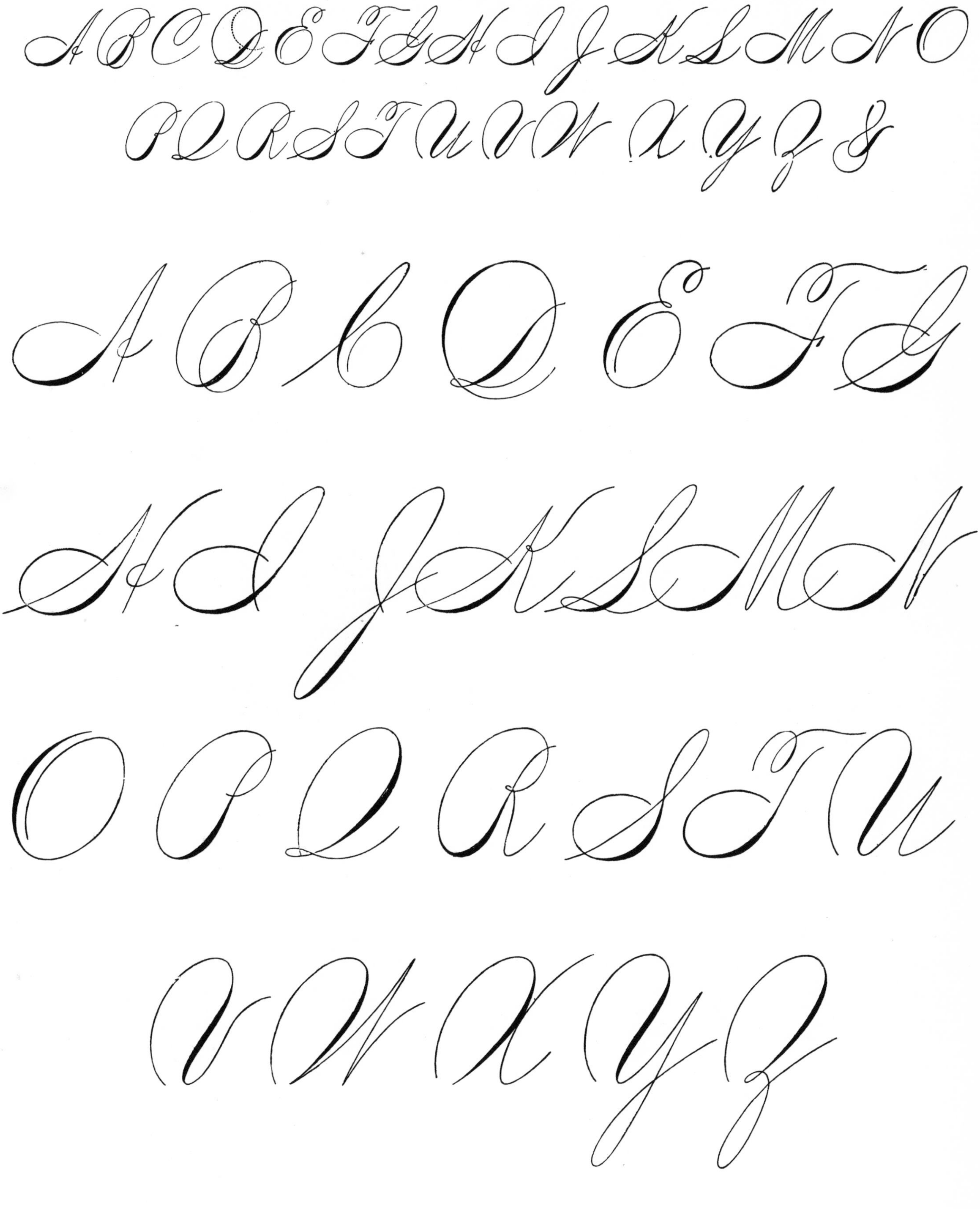

ABCDEFGHIJKLMN

OPQRSTUVWXYZ&

ABCDEFG

HIJKLMN

OPQRSTU

VWXYZ

a b c d e f g h i j k l

m n o p q r s t u v w x

y z & 1 2 3 4 5 6 7 8 9 0

A A B B C C D D E E

F F G G H H I I J J K K

L L M M N N O O P P Q Q

R R S S T T U U V V W

A B C D E F G H I J

K L M N O P Q R

S T U V W X Y Z

The first principle is the straight line.
The second principle is the right curve.
The third principle is the left curve.
The fourth principle is the extended loop, it is formed of the first two principles, as follows: Upward right curve three spaces, turn, and downward straight line crossing right curve one space wide and three spaces high.

The letter I consists of upward right curve one space high, downward straight line to ruled line, upward right curve, dot one space above letter. Analysis: Principles 2, 1, 2.

The letter U consists of the three lines of I with a repetition of the last two lines. It is one space high and one space wide and is used for measuring both the height and width of all written letters. Analysis: Principles 2, 1, 2.

The letter W consists of the letter U changed by making the third right curve one-half space nearer the straight line, and finish with a horizontal right curve. Analysis: Principles 2, 1, 2, 1, 2, 2.

The letter C consists of upward right curve, downward left curve one-sixth space, upward right curve, crossing right curve, downward left curve, upward right curve. Analysis: Principles 2, 3, 2, 3, 2.

The letter E consists of upward right curve, downward left curve, crossing right curve one-half space nearer from base line, turn, upward right curve. Analysis: Principles 2, 3, 2.

The letter R consists of upward right curve one and one-fourth space, downward left curve, downward straight line, upward right curve. Analysis: Principles 2, 3, 1, 2.

The letter S consists of upward right curve one and one-fourth space, downward compound curve, downward right curve. Analysis: Principles 2, 3, 2.

The letter N consists of upward left curve, upward right curve, downward straight line, upward right curve. Analysis: Principles 3, 1, 3, 1, 2.

The letter M is the same as N with a repetition of the last two lines. Analysis: Principles 3, 1, 3, 1, 2.

The letter V consists of upward left curve, downward straight line, upward right curve, horizontal right curve. Analysis: Principles 3, 1, 2, 2.

The letter X consists of the last two lines of M with a straight line on a slant of 40 degrees crossing first straight line at half the height. Analysis: Principles 3, 1, 2, 1.

The letter O consists of upward left curve, downward right curve, horizontal right curve. Analysis: Principles 3, 2, 1.

The letter A consists of upward left curve, downward straight line, upward right curve, downward straight line, upward right curve. Analysis: Principles 3, 1, 2, 1, 2.

The letter T consists of upward left curve, downward straight line, upward right curve, horizontal straight line, one and a half spaces from base line. Analysis: Principles 2, 1, 2.

The letter D consists of upward left curve, downward straight line, upward right curve, horizontal straight line, upward right curve. Analysis Principles 3, 3, 2, 1, 2.

The letter Q consists of the first three lines of A combined with downward straight line, upward compound curve. Analysis: Prin. 3, 3, 2, 1, 2, 3.

The letter P consists of upward right curve, downward straight line, upward left curve, downward straight line, upward right curve. Analysis: Principles 2, 1, 3, 1, 2.

The letter L consists of upward right curve, turn, downward straight line, upward right curve. Analysis: Principles 4, 2.

The letter B consists of upward right curve, downward left curve, upward straight line, horizontal right curve. Analysis: Principles 3, 2, 1.

The letter H consists of upward right curve, turn, downward straight line, upward left curve, downward straight line, upward left curve. Analysis: Principles 4, 3, 1, 3.

The letter K consists of upward right curve, turn, downward straight line, upward left curve, downward compound curve, upward right curve. Analysis: Principles 4, 3, 3, 2.

The letter J consists of upward right curve, downward straight line, turn, upward left curve. Analysis: Principles 2, 4.

The letter G consists of upward left curve, downward straight line, turn, upward right curve, downward straight line, turn and upward left curve.—Prin. 3, 3, 2, 4

The letter Y consists of upward left curve, downward straight line, upward right curve, downward straight line, upward left curve.—Prin. 3, 1 2, 4.

The letter Z consists of upward left curve, turn, downward right curve, downward right curve, upward left curve. Analysis. Principles 3, 2, 4.

The letter F consists of upward right curve, turn, downward straight line, turn, upward right curve, upward right curve. Analysis: Principle 4, 4, 2.

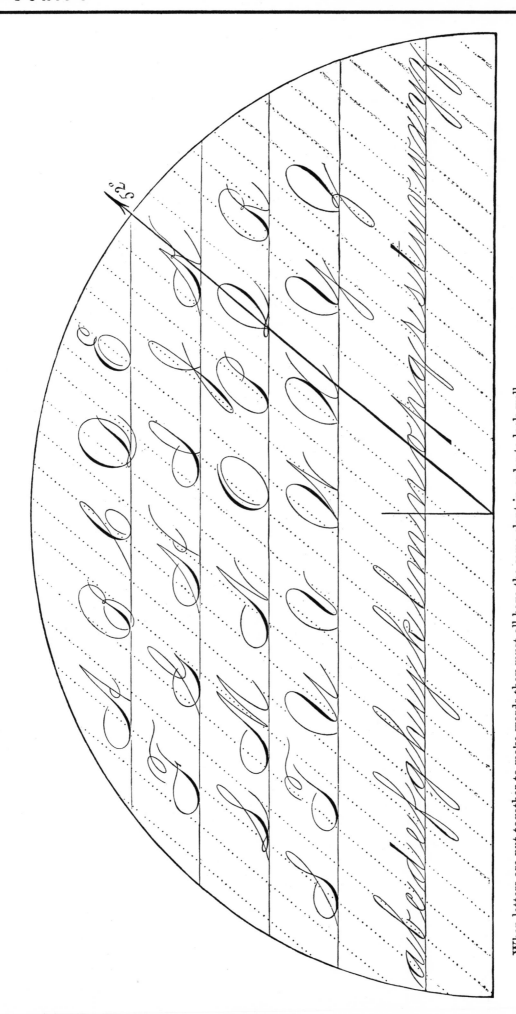

When letters are put together to make words they must all have the same slant in order to look well.

All good penmen agree that letters look the best when slanted about 52° (fifty-two degrees) from the horizontal, the same as you see them in the above cut.

By comparing the letters with the scale of slant, the same as you see in the above cut, you will see at once just how much to slant all the letters.

How much to slant letters is one of the first and most important things to learn.   By the use of the above cut and these instructions, it is also one of the easiest things to learn, for you can see at once, without any trouble at all, just how much to slant letters.

The first principle is called the *straight line* and is usually one space in length, and in all letters, except small x, has a slant of 52 degrees.

The second principle is called the *right curve* and is thus named because it is found on the right side of any oval figure. It is usually made on the *connective slant* of 30 degrees.

The third principle is called the *left curve* because found on the left of any oval figure. It is usually ide on the slant of 30 degrees.

The fourth principle is called the *extended loop* and is formed by the union of the first three principles, the second and third forming a loop crossing one space above base line and one-third the height of principle.

The fifth principle is called the *capital O*, and consists of left curve, broad turn, right curve, broad turn and left curve, terminating one-third space from baseline. Entire height, three spaces; entire width, two spaces; distance between left curves one-third space.

The sixth principle is called the *inverted oval* and consists of left curve, broad turn and right curve. Height three spaces; width at one-half the height, one and one-half spaces; at bottom, one-third space.

The seventh principle is called the *capital stem* and consists of a left curve, a right curve and a left curve, the last two forming oval, two and one-half spaces in length and one and one-half spaces in width. Slant of oval 15 degrees.

Capital *A* consists of capital stem joined angularly at top to a slight left curve extending divergently to base line and finished by left curve uniting with right, crossing first left curve one-half space above base line and terminating one space above.
Analysis: Principles 7, 3, 3, 2.

Capital *N* consists of the first two lines of A united by short curve at bottom to a left curve extending two spaces above base line. Distance between lines at half the height of letter should be equal.
Analysis: Principles 7, 3, 3.

Capital *M* consists of the first two lines of N joined by short turn to left curve extending upward three spaces, uniting angularly with left curve extending to base line, joining with short turn to a right curve extending upward one space. At half the height, three equal spaces.
Analysis: Principles 7, 3, 3, 2.

Capital *T* consists of the capital stem modified by being bent and shortened one-half space at top, over this is placed the cap of letter, consisting of left curve, inverted loop and left and right curve. At left of capital stem, three equal spaces. The cap should be made first.
Analysis: Principles 7, 3, 2, 3.

Capital *F* is formed the same as T, except that the last curve of the oval of capital stem is bent downward and extended upward across the capital stem, terminating with left curve downward one-half the height of letter downward one-fourth space.
Analysis: Principles 7, 3, 2, 3.

Capital *K* consists of the first two lines of H, to which is added a left and right curve uniting by loop at half the height of letter to a right and left curve joined on base line to a right curve terminating at head line.
Analysis: Principles 2, 7, 3, 2, 2, 3, 2.

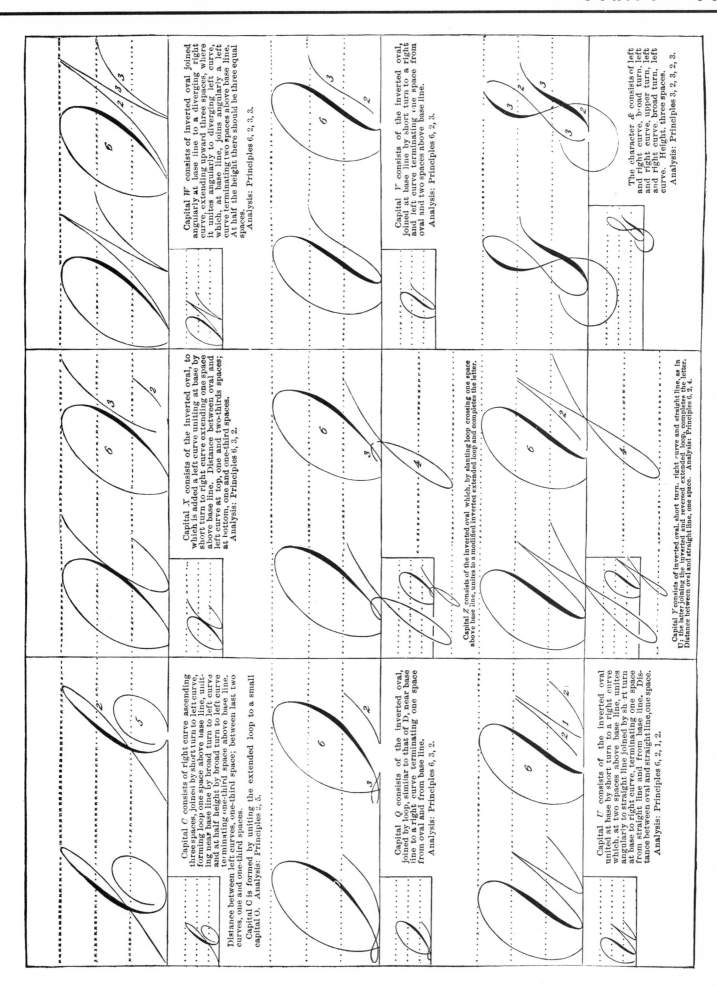

Capital C consists of right curve ascending three spaces, joined by short turn to left curve, forming loop one space above base line, uniting near base line by broad turn to left curve, and at half height by broad turn to left curve terminating one-third space above base line.

Distance between left curves, one-third space; between last two curves, one and one-third spaces.

Capital C is formed by uniting the extended loop to a small capital O. Analysis: Principles 2, 5.

Capital Q consists of the inverted oval, joined by short turn to that of D, near base line to a right curve terminating one space from base line.

Analysis: Principles 6, 3, 2.

Capital U consists of the inverted oval united at base by short turn to a right curve which, at two spaces above base line, unites angularly to straight line joined by short turn at base to right curve, terminating one space from straight line and from base line, Distance between oval and straight line, one space.

Analysis: Principles 6, 2, 1, 2.

Capital X consists of the inverted oval, to which is added a left curve uniting at base by short turn to right curve extending one space above base line. Distance between oval and left curve at top, one and two-thirds spaces; at bottom, one and one-third spaces.

Analysis: Principles 6, 3, 2.

Capital Z consists of the inverted oval which, by slanting loop crossing one space above base line, unites to a modified inverted extended loop and completes the letter.

Capital Y consists of inverted oval, short turn, right curve and straight line, as in U; the latter joining the inverted and reversed extended loop, completes the letter. Distance between oval and straight line, one space. Analysis: Principles 6, 2, 4.

Capital W consists of inverted oval joined angularly at base line to a diverging right curve, extending upward three spaces, where it unites angularly to diverging left curve, which, at base line, joins angularly a left curve terminating two spaces above base line. At half the height there should be three equal spaces.

Analysis: Principles 6, 2, 3.

Capital V consists of the inverted oval, joined at base line by short turn to a right and left curve terminating one space above oval and two spaces above base line.

Analysis: Principles 6, 2, 3.

The character & consists of left and right curve, broad turn, left and right curve, upper turn, left and right curve, broad turn, left curve. Height, three spaces.

Analysis: Principles 3, 2, 2, 3.

Capital *H* consists of left curve extending upward from base line two and one-half spaces, uniting angularly to a capital stem straightened at top; to this portion are added lines similar to the last two in A, except that the first of these has greater curvature at top. The portion of oval above dividing line is one and one-half times that below. Analysis: Principles 2, 7, 3, 3, 2.

Capital *P* begins two and one-half spaces above base line with first two curves of capital stem, uniting by broad turn to left curve ascending to full height of letter and uniting by broad turn to right curve, crossing first left curve two and one-third and one and one-half spaces above base line. Width of oval, one and one-half spaces; between capital stem and last right curve, one-half space. Analysis: Principles 7, 3, 2.

Capital *B* is formed like P, and has small loop crossing capital stem at right angles at half height of letter, joined to right curve, uniting one-fifth space below base line to left curve extending to one-half height of letter. Analysis: Principles 7, 3, 2, 2, 3.

Capital *R* is formed the same as R down to and including loop, from which it joins a right and left curve united by short turn at base line to a right curve terminating one space from base line. Analysis: Principles 7, 3, 2, 2, 3.

Capital *G* consists of right curve extending upward from base line three spaces, where it unites by short turn to left curve, crossing first curve one space above base line, and uniting by broad turn to a right curve, which joins angularly at half the height of letter, to the lower half of capital stem. Analysis: Principles 2, 3, 2, 3, 7.

Capital *S* consists of right curve extending from base line upward three spaces, united by short turn to capital stem, modified by increased curvature. The oval is divided similarly to H and K. Loop crossing one-half the height. Analysis: Principles 2, 7.

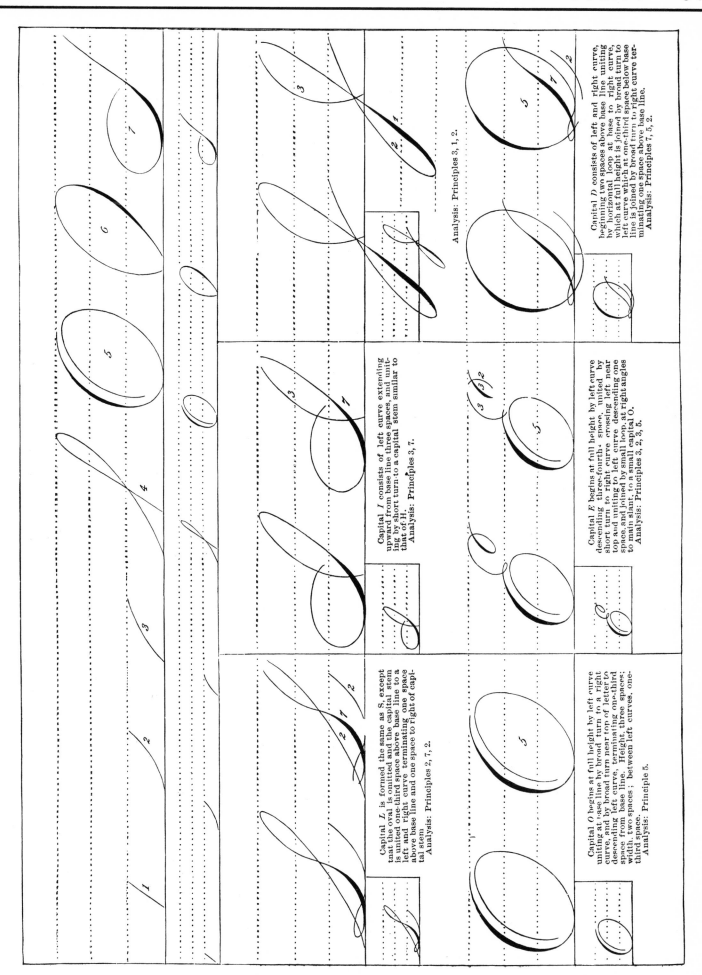

Capital *L* is formed the same as S, except that the oval is omitted and the capital stem is united one-third space above base line to a left and right curve, terminating one space above base line and one space to right of capital stem
Analysis: Principles 2, 7, 2.

Capital *O* begins at full height by left curve uniting at base line by broad turn to a right curve, and by broad turn near top of letter to descending left curve, terminating one-third space from base line. Height, three spaces, width, two spaces; between left curves, one-third space.
Analysis: Principle 5.

Capital *I* consists of left curve extending upward from base line three spaces, and uniting by short turn to a capital stem similar to that of H.
Analysis: Principles 3, 7.

Capital *E* begins at full height by left curve descending three-fourths space, united by short turn to right curve, crossing left near top and uniting to left curve descending one space, and joined by small loop, at right angles to main slant, to a small capital O.
Analysis: Principles 3, 2, 3, 5.

Analysis: Principles 3, 1, 2.

Capital *D* consists of left and right curve, beginning two spaces above base line uniting by horizontal loop at base to right curve, which at full height is joined by broad turn to left curve which at one-third space below base line is joined by broad turn to right curve terminating one space above base line.
Analysis: Principles 7, 5, 2.

Madame Feliciana Belleslettres respectfully announces that on Tuesday, September 5, she will resume initiating Young Ladies into the mysteries of Polite Bagatelle and Elegant Chitchat.   Room 39, Classic Building.

$478.07.   Nine days after date, I promise to pay to Graball Crunchem, Four Hundred and Seventy-eight Dollars and Seven Cents.

The pleasure of Mr. and Mrs. Guzzleton Turkeytongue's company is requested at Merryvale Hall, on Wednesday, 14th instant.   Dinner at five in the afternoon precisely.

Prof. Cramitin Boynoddles
Ancient University of Pantological Impossibles
Dr. Mr. Bought of Mr. Cr.
1234567890

Oilystone & Splitwhiskers
Self-Operating Razor-Strop Factory
1234567890

Blooming Grove Female Academy
Constitution-Tinkers and Law-Cobblers Association
Dr. Mr. Bought of Mr. Cr.
1234567890

Choice Productions of the Graver
This Series of Script Type is very Unique and Beautiful
Its Introduction Needs no Apology
1234567890

Science of Penmanship
Elegant Specimens of American Handwriting
Neatness, Grace and Dignity
1234567890

Epistolary Instruction
Progressive Lessons on Wielding the Pen
Bold Round Hands
12345678

Loveknot's Boarding-School
Matrimonial Aspirations Encouraged
Beauxtown Landing
1234567890

Rodman's Bombardier Field Practice
Finely Embellished by Numerous Forcibly Striking Illustrations
Arbitrament of Hundred Pounders
1234567890

National Popgun Institute!
Established in Sleekgabber Borough, April 1st, 1789
Academy of Humbugs
1234567890

Customary Spring Card to the Fashionable Public
Bazaar of Fashion, 1293 French Street
The Misses Lovelace Announce their Opening of Spring Bonnets
Perfection of Beauties in Parisian Styles
1234567890

Mr. & Mrs. Eliphalet Sugarheart
At Home, Thursday
Dr. Quack Killemgood, Autocratic Corn-Eradicator
Association of Amateurs of Ladyogling
1234567890

Recherche and Delightfully Select Literary Readings
Mother Goose has the pleasure to announce a Series of Choice Selections from her Popular Melodies
Tickets by Auction for Red Riding Hood and Blue Beard Nights

$689.37.   Philadelphia, April 1st, 1872.

Four months after date we promise to pay to the order of
Air, Sunshine & Co., Eighteen Tons and Fifty Bushels,
with interest, for value received.   Hay, Rye & Bro.

Cheatemwell Land Association

Fiddlestick Perpetual Fire Assurance Company

Gatling, Torpedo & Ironclad, Terrestrial Regulators,

Inform Aspirants for Power

That they are prepared to Subdue Refractory Tendencies in Humanity

Riotous or Revolutionary Demonstrations Effectually Quelled

Tottering Monarchies Permanently Propped

States Consolidated or Divided to suit the Convenience of their Patrons

Territory Conquered for the Highest Bidder

Kingdoms Provided in any Quarter of the World on Reasonable Terms.

Homes Desolated, Manhood Mangled, Countries Depopulated,

Or other Works of Destruction Speedily Executed on Special Order

Mrs Mr Dr Cr 1234567890 th &C Th Tl Wh

This Series of a New Style of Script, which we call Spencerian, we present to the attention of the Printers of the United States with an assured confidence that it will meet with their hearty approval. Its elegant appearance speaks more decidedly than any words; but we must state, that in addition to its great beauty, it possesses wearing qualities no less striking and important. While the hairlines are strongly supported by an adequate bevelled shoulder, the kerned ends are so well protected, that they will not readily snap off, but will stand as severe a pressure as the centre of the letter

Academy of Natural Sciences

Meeting for Promotion of Zoological Researches

Kangaroo, Flea, Natural Acrobats

Philadelphia, October 26, 1934.

One day after date I promise to deliver to my son Dick, on his bare back, for correctional purposes, ten strokes of a stout leathern strap, laid on with energy sufficient to prove to him my anxiety for his welfare.

Solomon Makeyoumind.

Joint=Stock Association

Protection of Soft-hearted Husbands

Annual Drive, Coaching Club.
Philadelphia to Everywhere.
Punctually at 7.30 A. M. November 4, 1878.
Seats Awarded the Week Preceding.
Horses en Route, Nov. 2.
Dinner at Mansion of Jehu Crackwhip.
Blue Coat, White Breeches, Red Vest

$951.00.   Bullionton, May 7, 1878.

Ten days after date I promise to pay
to the order of Grabwell & Holdfast, Nine
Hundred and Fifty-One Dollars, without
defalcation, for value received.

Nathan Outofcash.

Dearest Father . . . I am sure you will be glad to know of our safe arrival. We found Aunt Keziah well and cheerful, and Uncle bright as the morning and ruddy as a Spitzenberg. Mother enjoys the visit greatly; and as for me, I cannot express the sense of enjoyment I find in our relative's happy family. Your presence is alone wanting. Why will you continue a voluntary prisoner to the tyrant Business?

Your affectionate daughter
Ella Eglantine.

Mother Dear . . . Oh! the fun we have here at Grand= father's! Jennie and her cousin came here and we gave them a ride on our ponies; and they were not frightened a bit, but laughed till Stonytop's hounds began to bay! Love to you and Pop. No more from

Your loving son   Willie.

Dear Mother . . . I seek your advice on the grave subject of matrimony. On every visit to Grandpa's our pleasure was augmented by the presence of Tendersoul's daughter Amarilla. She is affectionate, industrious and religious. Have I your consent to ask permission of her parents to pay my addresses.

Your affectionate son, J. Dumpling Honeyheart.

This Certifies, That J. D. Honeyheart and A. S. Tendersoul were by me United in the Bonds of Matrimony, according to the Laws of Camden.

Sixth day of January, One Thousand Eight Hundred and Ninety.   Maritus Kempis, D. D.

Exchange for $9426.   Philadelphia, Dec. 7th, 1898.

At sight of this our Second of Exchange, (First and Third unpaid,) Pay to the Order of Thirstie McHunger &Co Nine Thousand Four Hundred and Twenty=Six Crullers, which charge to the account of   Goodfellow, Sayer &Co

Let this Certify, That F. Schœffer Gutenberg is a Member of the Philadelphia Typographical Society. May, 1895.   A. Compositor, President.

Seventeenth International Convocation

Association for Encouraging Habits of Industry

Pledge on Initiation of Members

Knowing that the Human Hand, intelligently educated and skilfully employed, has rescued man from Barbarism, and made his position far superior to that of animals not possessing this useful appendage, also believing that it can, by judicious use, still further Elevate humanity and Lighten the Burdens yet weighing heavily on some of its unfortunate sons, I therefore

Hereby Faithfully Covenant

That my hands, as well as those of others placed under my care, shall be perfectly instructed in some Handicraft beneficial to the race, and that I will on all occasions endeavor to keep them fully employed in works of use or beauty, and will refrain from uplifting them in any way that may injure my fellows or mar the fair face of Nature.

May 26, 1987.

Philanthropic Busybody.

Meetings for Nomination

Patent Law-Making Machine
Constitutions and Enactments Ground out with Despatch
Preventive of Lobbying, Bribery, Logrolling
1234567890

Corner in the Umbrella Market
Wet-Weather Perpetual
Consultation of Bulls and Old Probability
1234567890

Cars Propelled by Nitro-Glycerine
Rapid Transit Problem

Universal Debt Cancellation
Repudiation League

Maiden Supporting Grandmamma's Footsteps
Beauty Gracefully Bending

Lunatics in Solemn Conspiracy
Philosophic Pismires Attacking Granite Foundations
Entombed Beneath a Falling Pebble
1234567890

Discoveries of Scientism!
Worship Him, ye Pantheistic Wiseacres!
Molecule, Evolution, Protoplasm!
1234567890

Pennies Appropriated by Peculators
Poorfolk's Savings Bank

Laughed at by Plain Folks
Strutting Pomposity

Redeeming Promises in the World's

Currency National Bank of Performance

Practical Penmanship.

Bills Receivable. Cash Cr.

New York Writing-School.

D. Daniel T. Ames. & Co

Umbrella Borrowing Society

Grand International Topographical

Conclave.

Scaramouches' Nocturnal Parade.

Historical Marginalia.

MEANDERING CLUB AND GADABOUT CO.

MODERN WIFEHOOD

HAT MEN'S CLUB

HONORARY MEMBERSHIP

ANNUAL TRADE SALES

HINE DRESS FABRICS

KNIGHTS OF THE TEMPLE

SMASHER EXPRESS

Trunk Demolishing Scientifically Executed

PREMIUM

National Bank of the Republic

PANNIER-BACK

BUNCHINESS

SNEEZERS

RUFFLE

RUBBER COATING

Demimonde's Patent Blush Varnish

BEARDEDNESS
Handsome Ruggedness
Nature's Stamp
1234567890

DAYBEAMS
Universal Freedom
The Press
1234567890

TRUTH-GATE
Guarded by Innocence
Tremulous

MANHOOD'S CONQUERORS
Maidenhood Smiling, Womanhood Weeping

BLOOD HEAT
High Season and Low Reason
12345678

DREAMINGS
Dimples before Wrinkles
12345678

JEWELER

FRIDAY EVENING CONCERT

1234567890

AUTUMN

NATIONAL EXPLOIT

1234567890

MEDICAL DIPLOMA

WINTER PASTIMES

EXPEDITIOUS

THROUGH RAILROAD

12345678

RELIABLE

BROAD ROADS

123456

NIGHT LINE

WEIGHTS

DISPATCHES

IRONBOUND VAULT
Protector of Economy's Accumulations

COMFORTER
Automatic Housecleaning Machine

MUTUAL INSURANCE
Neighbourly Association for Common Protection

Lilies and Daffadowndillies
Wildflower Specimens from the Forest
1234567890

Panoramic Changes
Fine Architectural Decoration
1234567890

College of Physicians

Hospital Graduates   Medical Inventions

MAGPIE'S HIDING PLACES
Point-Lace, Ruffles, Cuffs, Trinkets, Broken Crockery
1234567890

GARRET RAMBLES
Looking-up Grandfather's Curious Oddities
1234567890

SURVIVAL OF THE FITTEST
Good Children Early Made Angels, Devil's Servants Centennarians

PROGRESS OF SCIENCE
Professor Tinderdale's Short March to Materialism
1234567890

CRYING NECESSITY
Legal Muzzles for Smutmouth Scribblers
1234567890

FREE LOVERS, ATTENTION
Hundredth Annual Meeting at Tittletattle's Assembly Rooms

EGYPTIAN ARTIFICE
CREDULITY   SERVITUDE

Arabian Literary Remains

SUMMER MORNING'S DEW-DROPS

Sparkling Gleams on Beauty's Laughing Cheek

Pendant Crystals

AMUSING LECTURES
WANDERINGS AMONG BARBARIANS
1234567890

OSTENTATIOUS
SUNFLOWER DECORATION
1234567

DIAMOND BOSOM-STONES

BRIGHT SPARKS GARDEN BOUQUET

Treachery and Ingratitude
Barbed Spears that Wound their Perpetrators
1234567890

Undoubted Millionaires
Blessed Ones at Peace with Heaven
1234567890

Unnerving Wild Sensations

Overwork and Hunger

Inseparable Companions

EXHAUSTIVE TREATISE ON BLEEDING
Flagellatory, Pugilistic, Duelistic, Homicidal, Suicidal, Tonsorial, Financial
Valuable to Sharpers and Men-about-town

NOCTURNAL BANQUETS
Morning Headache and Breakfast-Table Snappishness

✻SUBTERRANEOUS✦SEPULCHRES✻
✦ENTOMBING✦REMAINS✦   ✦PRIMITIVE✦MARTYRS✦
✻VOICELESS✦CATACOMBS✻

✻MINERALOGICAL✦ENTERPRISE✻
⚊SILVER✦MINING⚊   ⚊COPPER✦DIGGING⚊
✻GOLD✦DUST✦PANNING✻

TOURNAMENTS
Cavaliers in Martial Furbelows

INFLUENCE ON HEALTH AND WEALTH
LANIFEROUS ANIMALS

BICYCLE + OMNIBUS + COMPANY
STEAM SUPERSEDED

PERAMBULATOR COMPANY
PALANQUINS, + SEDAN-CHAIRS, + VELOCIPEDES

MISCHIEVOUS + MEDDLING
REGULATING KITCHEN DOMESTIC ECONOMY

BELLICOSE BARRISTERS
PERPLEXING + LABYRINTH + OF + LITIGATION
1234567890

REGIMENT + DRILLING
BRILLIANT MILITARY MOVEMENT
1234567890

CERAMIC RESEARCHES
CURIOUSLY + DECORATED + GRECIAN + POTTERY

PICKAXE AND SHOVEL GYMNASTICS
EXCAVATING FOR CURIOSITIES AT HERCULANEUM

OLYMPIAN TRAINING SCHOOL
YOUTHFUL REGIMEN FOR MUSCULAR DEVELOPMENT

Knockers, Spinners and Expert Catchers

Nightly Foraging Rambles

Industrious and Skilled Mechanics

⧫DISREPUTABLE⧫ENTERPRISE⧫
⧫Betting⧫on⧫Elections⧫   ⧫Cornering⧫the⧫Market⧫

⧫INCOMPREHENSIBLE⧫
⧫Partisan⧫Tactics⧫of⧫Political⧫Ringsters⧫

ARABESQUE ORNAMENTS
Gathered from the Courts of Oriental Potentates

Notice from Managers of Asylum for Cranks
Shallow=brained, Giddy=headed Buzzards and Dithyrambic Wiseacres
Admitted without Certificate upon Personal Application

Extravagant Bachelor's Contemplated Reformation
Assisted by Submissive Maiden with Banknotes in Profusion

1234567890

Dephlegmate and Anhydrous
Mackintoshes, Waterproofs and Galoches

Celebrating the Landing of our Forefathers

Herdsman and Plowshare

SOCIAL CUSTOMS IN ANCIENT PALMYRA
AUXILIARY MECHANICAL APPLIANCES OF THE PYRAMID BUILDERS
WANDERINGS OF THE TROUBADOURS

But, while Benefiting us, it may be a Charity to many
half-naked unfortunates.   Our store is piled up with
Neatly-fitting Clothing, made of high-grade material.
We want to get rid of it, and ask you to carry away
enough for your use: you can do so for a mere song

WE MEAN BUSINESS NOT CHARITY

∴ 1 2 3 4 5 6 7 8 9 0 ∴

Useless Lying on our Shelves
While ∴ Rags ∴ are ∴ Perambulating ∴ the ∴ Streets

DRESS * LIKE * NABOBS

And your friends will do you reverence!
Step up to our Counter and we will
load you down with Garments that
will Elevate you in Social Circles

∴ 1 2 3 4 5 6 7 8 9 0 ∴

* * *

Shabby Arrivals
Depart ∴ in ∴ Princely ∴ Costume

LATTER-DAY + EXCRESCENCES

Professional + Personators + Signature + Imitators

UNCOMMON MUSCULAR STRETCHINGS
Lady Skaters' Rink Carnivals, Fashionable Back Breakers
1234567890

INTERESTED COSMOPOLITANS
Government Contracts, Politicians' Pulse Warmers

ZOOLOGICAL RESEARCHES
Slimshank Mountain-Necked Camelopardus

MARCH WINDS AND APRIL SHOWERS

AGRICULTURAL PREPARATIVES   HORTICULTURAL ASSISTANTS

HIGHWAY CLEANERS AND HOUSE VENTILATORS

MORNINGWALK & CHEERFULFACE
FAMILY PHYSICIANS
1234567890

QUESTIONS OF AVOIRDUPOIS
FREIGHT CHARGES

PROMOTIVE OF INDUSTRIAL ENTERPRISE
LETTER-PRESS PRINTING

COMMERCIAL CORPORATIONS
PERAMBULATORS

TELEGRAPHIC DISPATCHES
NEWSPAPERDOM

SURROUNDINGS OF CONTAMINATION

PESTILENTIAL INFLUENCES DEPRAVED ASSOCIATIONS

1234567890

VESSELS IN DISTRESS

EMPTY PLATTERS   BROKEN DISHES

DIFFICULT NAVIGATION
STARTING OUT WITH SCHOONERS

INDICATIONS
GRAND STORM MATINEE

RAMMING EXPLOIT

FLASHY BIPEDS

PICKLED MOONSHINE

ARTILLERY

THUNDERINGS

UNCHIDING LECTURES
Sharper than Stinging Recrimination
Keenly Cutting

BRIGHTER PROSPECT
Morning Light Succeeding Night
Good Signs

CREEPING CREEKS   SUNNY MARCE

WINDING RAILROADS

CHEERFUL MORNING GLIMMERS   CONSPICUOUS

SLANTING EVENING BEAM   SPLINTERED

NOONTIDE GLEAMING   IRON-BOUND

FRINGED CLOUD   BLUNTED

POLITICAL DECENCIES
Fossil Specimens from
Ancient Quarries

MOON'S EXTRACT
Excellent for Polite Fiddlefaddles

REFRESHING   **PROMISING**
SUMMER MORNINGS   **COMING SPRING**

HUMORSOME   SHADOWS

EXTEND STORM

BUNKERS

→BEAUTIFUL × FLORENCE←
→Jubilant Bells Ringing Merrily in Festive Seasons←
→Ivy-covered Towers of Merrie England←

→EDITORIAL ⚜ ADDRESS←
→Comfort and Refinement Precursor←
→Profitable Intellect←

LADIES' BALMORAL FRINGINGS
1234567890

CONTRACT FOR FORTUNE
1234567890

MONKISH LIMNINGS

PITCHFORKING

HUCKLEBACK

LAKELET

ABRUPT CURVES

THORNBUD

SKUNK'S COMPOUND
Highly Fashionable Deodorizer
1234567890

COURAGEOUS
Champagne Epicureans
12345678

NECESSITIES   MEMBERSHIP

BURSTED   SCHEMES

SEQUENT

HANDSOME PORTRAITS
PENCIL SKETCHES

CROOKED QUESTIONS
MERRIMENT

SQUARE DEALING
EXPECTED

COMMON LUXURIES
ARGENTIFEROUS KITCHEN-WARES
HARD-METAL BAKEPANS
1234567890

OBLITERATION
CURTAINED WINDOWS
DARKENING

MAGNETIC
COUNTENANCES

STUPIDLY SEEKING REPOSE
Banisters Creaking
Sneaking Toes-Stumper and Creeping Nose-Bumper
1234567890

CAUSING GENERAL TERROR

Children Crying, Wife Sighing,

Comfort Dying Sorrowful Household

JUDICIAL DOCUMENTS

Legal Process   Musty Rulings

TRIUMPHANT

Elevation   Triangles

KINDLING-WOOD
Adapted to firing Quick Tempers

BANKRUPTCY
Occidental Wine Company

BRUMMELL MUDGINS
Physiognomical Hairdresser in General

KITCHEN HALLS
Rare Pictures of the Imagination
RULER OF THE ROAST

IMMACULATE
Blissful Dreams of Utopia
CHEATING OBSOLETE

SATANIC CONFLICTS
Heaven's Wonderfully-Made Handiwork
CRUSHED AND MANGLED

DECADENCE OF AUTHORITY
IRON CLAD OATHS

SHADES OF OPINION

MIRRORED REFLECTION
SHIMMERING WINDBLOWN WAVELETS

ILLUMINATION
SUMMER AURORAL GLEAMS

STATISTICAL INFORMATION

FINANCIAL TACTICS

FOR HYPOTHECATORS

MONEY MARKET

BUSINESS RECUPERATION

BICENTENNIAL
Congratulatory Orations
1234567890

PROBITY
Deposit Institution

ECCENTRICITY
Punctuality, Truthfulness

DEMENTED DARWINIANS
CRACK-BRAINED

SPRING CAMPAIGN
WANDERING

OCCIDENTAL CRUSADERS
GENTLE VIOLENCE

FACING THE ENEMY

SHARP AS HORNET-STING
PORCUPINISH LAW

THE PEOPLE'S VOICE
SURRENDERED

Infant Blossoms
BLOOMING

Home=Cradled Youngsters
GARNERINGS

PATENTED
FLUNKEY KNEE-OIL
123456

CORONET
NOBLE SPIRITS
123456

HEAD-BOBBING
GENTEEL NINCOMFOOLS
123456

MECHANISM
Patent Talkative Tinfoil

COMPENDIUM OF TRICKINESSES
Showing how to Attain Efficiency in the Art of Men-Managing
Selections from the Diary of a Lady of Leisure

GRANDFATHERS' CONVENTION
Contributions from the Memory-Book of Patriarchs
Experience Meeting at Eventide

LESSONS IN SMOKING
Juvenile Martyrs' Behaviour under Fire
Dissensions in Stomach Region

BUSINESS SPECTROSCOPE
Fine Metals Undiscoverable in Bank Vaults

Sprouting Cherubs
BUDDINGS

HUNTING SCENE
Dangerous Adventures

SUBURBAN DISTURBANCE
MORNING DISCORDS   EVENING SERENADE

NORTHERN PROVINCE
CONTINUOUS ICEBERG ENVIRONMENT

ENORMOUS RESOURCE

FAIRMAID & CHAMPION
STAR GAZERS AND MOONSHINERS
COTTAGE BALCONY FAIRYDALE

UNPRINCIPLED MISCREANTS

CONDUCTORS

Unanimously Decided by the Members
Manifold Blessings follow in the Footsteps of Wisely-directed Industry
Windy Declamation often has Unfortunate Results

Blatant Rhetoric Discounted at Bank of Common Sense

Usefulness Commands Recognition

Unobtrusive · Specimens · of · Benevolence

Opulence and Penury Walking Arm-in-Arm

Missionaries Labouring among Politicians

· 1 2 3 4 5 6 7 8 9 0 ·

Thoroughly Acquainted with Family History

Retailer of Gossip Probable and Improbable

Counsellor in Matters Trivial or Momentous

Author and Publisher of Fictitious Incidents

Banging · Association · of · Calithumpia

Kettle-Drums and Locomotive Whistles

MODERN VICIOUS LITERATURE
Corrupting the Morals   Debasing our Citizens
Society for Suppression of Honest Industry
1234567890

MUSTACHE PROPAGATION
Watchful Solicitude of Juvenile Cultivators
1234567890

SOLITARY · RAMBLES · IN · SEARCH · OF · THE · PICTURESQUE
MOUNTAIN · STREAMS · AND · FAIRY · VALES

MORNING · TWILIGHT · FAINTLY · GLEAMING
PERFUMED · LOVE-LETTERS

FLOATING · OVER · THE · BILLOWS
SEASIDE · MUSINGS

WOMAN EMANCIPATORS, JACKET AND TROUSERS
RIDICULOUS EXPECTATION

DRUNKARD'S PROMENADE, ELECTION PRECINCTS
MONONGAHELA ARGUMENTS

FEMININE PALLADIUM, TONGUE UNBRIDLED
ROISTERING STATESWOMEN

GARDENS WATERED
CARRIAGE-WAYS SPRINKLED
DESERTS DRENCHED

SAINT SWITHIN
ABDICATES CONTROL

GROUND SATURATED
CRANBERRY BOGS IRRIGATED

THUNDER SHOWERS
PROTRACTED OR TEMPORARY

SURGING STREAMS

FIFTEEN MINUTES AT PYRAMID OF CHEOPS
Daylight Views of Sand-clad Plains, Ruined Temples and Mummy Tombs

MONUMENTS OF NINEVEH
Noontide Rambles amid Crumbling Buildings

ROMANTIC MEMORIES
Eating Dinner with Sphinx and Centaur

Mozambique MOUNTAINS

Ornamental Window-Shade Manufacturers
FABRICATE AND DECORATE

Printing-Office Enigma and Compositor Puzzler
UNREADABLE MANUSCRIPT

Ocean-Current & Thunder-Storm
UNIVERSAL LAUNDRY

Delusive MERCANTILE Operator

Virtuous Indignation of the Feminine Community
Constitutional Amendment Prohibiting the Manufacture and Sale of Mirrors
1234567890

Unprecedented Attractiveness
Travelling Circus Street Parades and the Latest Style of Millinery

Astronomical Bombardment
Fourth-of-July Pyrotechnical Displays

Homogeneous Noblemen
Caucasian, Ethiopian and Mongolian

INFORMATION WANTED
Conspicuous Newspaper Advertisement
1 2 3 4 5 6 7 8 9 0

CHARMING PROSPECT
Juvenile Cogitations on Maturity
1 2 3 4 5 6 7 8 9 0

EXPERIMENTAL
Neighborly Chitchat Analyzed

DISTRACTED
Mountebanks Bewildered

QUAINT COSTUMES
Promenading Thronged Sidewalks

VERNAL EQUINOX
Contagious Springtide Lassitude

A B C D E F G H I J K L M N O P Q R S T U V W X Y Z

MOONBEAMS DOWN THE ALLEYS

SPECTACLED GRANDMOTHERS

POLITICAL TORTUOSITIES

MIDSUMMER MIDNOON BEAMS

SHEPHERD & CROOK, MERCERS

FAIR FAT AND BUMPY

FANCIFUL HUMOURS

WORM-EATEN BROWNSTONE

MELTING AWAY IN THE FERVID RAY

BUSKINS FOR YOUNGSTERS

MERRILY-TWINKLING STARS

PRONGED SLANDERING TONGUES

TUMBLING BACKWARD

SUNBEAM PEERING THROUGH

EXCEEDING BEAUTIFUL

DEFINED BOUNDARIES

DECIDEDLY BORED

FORTIFIED STRONGHOLDS

WATER-DRIFTED MOSSES

MAGNIFICENT OCEAN VIEWS

FAIR INTELLECTUAL COUNTENANCE

SLENDER HEAD AND HEELS

DESCENDING LIGHTS

TUMBLING BRICKS BOYISH TRICKS

NOLI ME TANGERE

MOUNTAIN-SLOPES

PITILESS STORM

NUMSKULL BREAKERS

FEDERAL STATES

LIGHT WITHIN THE HABITATION

HANDSOMENESS

UPCLIMBING CLOUDS

BEAUTY'S OWN

FROLICKSOME

DRIPPING ROCKS UNDER THE FALL

PURE ELEGANCE

ROCK CRYSTALS

STAR-GIRDLED

MORNING STAR

SEABEATEN SHORE

SEED-DROPPING

IMPRISONMENT

SUBMERGED BENEATH

CHERUBIC WITCHES

MUGS OF MILK

CURLY-HEADED

TRANSLUCENT WATER

COMING MORN

STARS AND STRIPES

CONFOUNDED

STARRY LANTERNS

FRAGRANT BOUQUET

UNPRETENDING

ZIGZAG PATHS

BONED DANDIES

OUTPOURING

QUEER EXPERIMENTS

LOOKING UP

REFULGENCE

EMINENCE

PEELING BARK

BUNOLEO

REFLECTED

SHEPHERDS' CROOKS

PATENT EFFICACIOUS MANNER-POLISH

CHARACTER EXTINGUISHER

TERPSYCHOREAN

MELPOMENIC

CHILL WINTER'S LEAFLESS BOWERS

HERCULEAN ERINIC SHILLALEHS

SPIKEM AND SKEWER

CLUBS AND SPEARS

GUMPTION, FORTUNE-MAKER

PEACHES AND TOMATOS

CHARACTER PRESERVER

BUDDING BLOSSOMS

FIBBER'S TELEGRAM

PORK AND BEANS

MINNESINGERS

MELON SEEDS

FLEETHEEL'S WINGED VELOCIPEDES

FLYINGFISH AND FEATHERFOWL

WHIRLIGIGS AND WEATHERCOCKS

FLOWER LANGUAGE SIGHING LOVERS' LINGO

LAUGHING MAIDEN'S GAMBOLS

MIRTHFUL PROVOCATIONS

BORDER EDGINGS

SUN-TIPPINGS

METEORS

HOOKED

NATURE'S INCOMPARABLE HANDICRAFT

INFALLIBLE SKIRT-SUPPORTERS

SOMNIFEROUS NIGHTCAPS

PARISIAN SHOESTRINGS

ORNATE ALPHABET

NEEDLEGUN PUNCTURES

ENCHASED SAPPHIRES

DANGLE DINGLE DAISIES

FLASHES FROM RAVEN EYES

BEAUTIFUL GOLDEN GEM

FORTUNE'S FAVOURS

BEAUTY'S SLAVE

MODEST JEWEL

MOSSFRINGED BROOKSIDES

FAIR TURKISH SULTANA

CRICKET WHANGERS

WHORTLEBERRY

PRETTY DAMSEL

DIVERTISEMENTS
MUSICAL.

J. CONNER & SON.
$ 1234567890 £

COMPANION
MUSEUM.

LIBERTY
SHADE

HOLIDAY GIFTS
PICTORIAL.

GALLERY OF
PAINTINGS

DAWN OF MORNING
TWILIGHT.

THE OLD OAK TREE
1234567890

BEAUTIES OF NATURE
CULTIVATION.

INSTRUMENT.
WESTERN.

EGYPT AND ITS MONUMENTS,
VOYAGE UP THE NILE.

BUNKER HILL
MONUMENT.

FEMALE POETS OF
AMERICA.

ROSY DAWN OF LIGHT
$ 1234567890

INDEPENDENT
REPUBLIC

IMMORTALITY OF
THE SOUL.

THE CLOUDS AT EVENING DRIVEN

POND LILIES OILY-LEAVED AND PALE.

RISING TO MEET THEE.

YEARS ARE BEARING US TO HEAVEN,

NEW FACES GREET THEE

AT MEMORY'S MAGIC SIGN

HOME OF HAPPINESS AND REST

RIPPLING WATER MIRRORS

REVERBERATING ECHOES!

HUGE WATER OAK AND PINE

SILVER STREAMLET

FORESHADOW

ANGULAR

BARE IONIC COLUMN

GEMMED EYE

DELIGHTING

MAGNIFICENT

MARBLEIZED

HANDSOMER

INTERLINING

SUPERNACULUM

FRINGED

CAMELOPARDIANAS

INK-LIMNING

WATER-IMAGED

MELODIOUS

DIAMONDS

MELONS

OCCIDENT

RIGHT STRIPE

ELABORATE

ROPE ONIONS

ENTWINING

LIGHT ALOFT

SURROUNDED

EAVESDROPS

STRAWY

GLIMMERING

SOLID BLOCKS

ENCLOSURES

SPILLED

PANSIES

MIDSHIPS

MYSTIFIED

ZIGZAG

SPRING

STREAM

BENDING

ETCHING

SWAYING

SUMMER

LIKE MEMNON'S MUSIC OF OLD TIME

Mutual Insurance Company of New York.

TANGLED GROWTH OF VINE.

FAINT EVENING CHIMES

WANING MOON.

GLORIOUS ORB OF LIGHT

THE LOOSE IVY DANGLING.

GRIM SHADOWY FORM.

THE VIOLET NESTLING LOW

THE SPREADING FOLIAGE

AN AUTUMNAL SKY

A SNOW SCENE.

THE RAINBOW

RAIN DROPS.

THE CHIMES.

UPON THE HILLS

AT MIDNIGHT HOUR

MAY Queen.

HERE ARE OLD TREES, TALL OAKS, AND GNARLED PINES,

HEADLEY'S SACRED SCENES AND CHARACTERS.

JOURNAL OF THE PILGRIMS AT PLYMOUTH, IN 1620

PRESCOTT'S HISTORY OF THE CONQUEST OF PERU

LANDSCAPE GARDENING AND RURAL ARCHITECTURE

GOOD COUNSEL IS ABOVE PRICE.

COSTUME OF THE ANCIENTS

LEAVES FROM THE NOTE BOOK OF A NATURALIST

WANDERINGS OF A PILGRIM IN THE ALPS

FAMILY PICTURES.

UPCLIMBING WINDOW CREEPERS

MODEST MORNING·GLORIES

TOUCHES OF GENIUS

ADORNMENTS

BLOSSOMING

RIBBONED

WREATHS

Saturday Confab of Nymphs of the Washpave

Barbecue to Honour our Noble Townsman

Return of Josephus T. Capstone, Esquire

Mandates of Supreme Council

Daughters of Penelope

Tuesday Evening Jubilee

THE PETERSBURG INTELLIGENCER,
KENTUCKY. OHIO. MISSOURI.
$ 1234567890 &

WASHINGTON CITY,

RICHMOND WHIG.

$ 1234567890 &

RICHMOND STAR,

CUMBERLAND.

$ 1234567890

VENETIAN SERENADE

PICTURESQUE SKETCHES

SHADED.

BORDERS

ARCADIAN SKY

FIRMAMENT

FLOWERS

BEAUTIFUL

MORNING

ENGLAND

FRESCH

EMBELLISHING.

GLANE

MATHEMATICAL. 18

HALYARDS!

OCTAGON

AMERICA!

OUTLINES

THASLON

POETICAL

CONIDIN

ILLUSTRIOUS.

MEMORY

FOLIAGE

STREW

RENT

NICE

ROMAN

THOR

PENNSYLVANIA'S CARBON MOUNTAIN GEMS

ANCIENT METALLIFEROUS DEPOSITES

COMPENSATION IN ALTITUDE FOR LACK OF AMPLITUDE

IMAGINATION'S HIGHEST REACH

IMPENDING DARKNESS

CEDAR SHINGLES

INDISSOLUBLE

PARTNERSHIP

CHARCOAL MERCHANT

MOUNTAINEERS

BALTIMORE RAIL
ROAD. 1844

NEWBURG TELEGRAPH.
$1234567890£

BUFFALO DAILY ADVERTISER.
$1234567890£

WEATHERSFIELD,
BALTIMORE.

HUMAN

ELDON

WYOMING!

REPUBLIC
abiefghimy

ROLIN
DEBT-
MAYN
waine?

MILTON

ABCDEF

MODE

SALE

HER

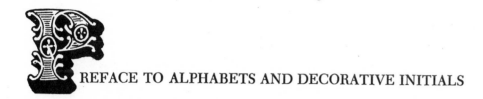

PREFACE TO ALPHABETS AND DECORATIVE INITIALS

All of us have some interest in decorative initials. We remember them from the fabulous books of our childhood, or we have seen them in the present-day books that we give to our own children. They come to us, really, out of the ancient days of legend and fable. Much of the charm, the fascination, of the medieval book lies in the use of initials to ornament and emphasize the text; and it is mostly from this period of book production that all later artists, type-designers and letter-designers have derived their inspiration for ornamental letters.

It was just at the end of the Middle Ages that the printing art came into startling and sudden importance as a producer of books. The manuscript writers, illuminators, and rubricators were faced with a competition that they were unable to overcome. For some time manuscripts and printed books were produced side by side. Of course, the printed book had to resemble the manuscript in most respects; and the student of early books knows this well. One of the concessions that many of the first printers made was to allow areas for the insertion of initials and illumination, which were to be put into the book by hand. It is clear that decorative initial usage followed an unbroken tradition from the manuscript book over into the first output of the printing-press. This is the point to be noted in even the slightest study of initial letters.

As the printer took over more and more of book production, it must have seemed foolish to him not to print the initials too. He therefore began to devise initials, cut in wood or type metal, which could be printed along with the text or stamped in separately in other colors. These ornamented letters, within the limitations imposed by the typographic process, were exactly what the Gothic initial artist had been drawing or painting into books for many generations. The lily-of-the-valley initials of Günther Zainer, which start the special collection of ornamental alphabets in this book, illustrate the derivation very well. They are fairly close to being the first set of decorative, typographic initials; they have been copied and "swiped" right up to the present day; and they may well serve us as a springboard from which to take off on this investigation of ornamented initials.

The other powerful stream of influence that affected all ornament and decoration was the Renaissance. The German printers who went into the Italian area to start presses there soon found that they had to produce type and initials to follow the style of the humanist manuscript. Printers such as Ratdolt, therefore, designed initials with a somewhat different flavor. The example of his initials shows a design which, again, has been copied over and over. It is not altogether by accident that Ratdolt is called the father of decorative typographic initials.

A third kind of initial was the illustrated or historiated letter. This style is very well shown in the examples of woodcut alphabets in our selection. It is amazing how much could be pictured in these little backgrounds for initial letters. Even great artists like Holbein and Dürer found in such a series of initials a most interesting and challenging project.

To skip lightly over history and influence is the final task of this introduction. The continuation of the Renaissance and the center of fine book production was situated in the French area during the first half of the 16th century. Sets of initials by Geoffroy Tory and other designers again set up an influence that has lasted into modern times, in the work of Frederic Goudy, Bruce Rogers, and others. The Low Countries took precedence in book and typographic production during the 17th century; and the tradition of decorative letters was continued, along with the introduction of engraved initials. Each area of western Europe, in its own time, produced series of decorative alphabets with which to ornament and enliven the typographic page.

Craftsmanship declined over the centuries. The 18th-century English book was nothing to brag about until John Baskerville displayed his examples of clean, chaste book production. But he left out all initials that could be called decorative. Here was started the movement against the use of the ornamented initial in books—at least against the traditional decorated letter.

With the development of lithography in the 19th century the type foundries were faced with a great competitor—for the lithographer could draw any and all sorts of letters on his stone; his imagination was free to roam, and it did. The type foundries took up the challenge, however, and produced during the 19th century a volume of ornamented types and alphabets that might be said to stagger the imagination. Fantastic is a mild word for many of these creations. In the latter part of this section devoted to initials, there have been included enough specimens to show the range of the 19th-century typographic fancy. These are the "Victorian," "Americana," etc.—ornamented types that went into the books and advertising that our grandfathers and great-grandfathers looked at.

It is hoped that in this addition to the history of early advertising typography the student or designer will find an exposition of that most important factor, the ornamented initial. What he must recall in looking at the 19th-century productions is that they were designed under the two main revival influences of the period: the Gothic and Renaissance revivals, especially in England. Any brief perusal of the examples shown will confirm this view. As for the fantastic, almost surrealistic, typographic concoctions of this whole era, one must regard them as the products of certain whimsical, sentimental, and sometimes psychotic elements in the then-prevailing European character. We in America were a part of this chain of typographic development. We imported type and type-designers to develop our own industry and service our budding advertising business.

1956   Alexander Nesbitt

The famous lily-of-the-valley alphabet used by Günther Zainer
at Augsburg, about 1475

Some of Erhard Ratdolt initials, showing use of italianate ornament,
1476-1486

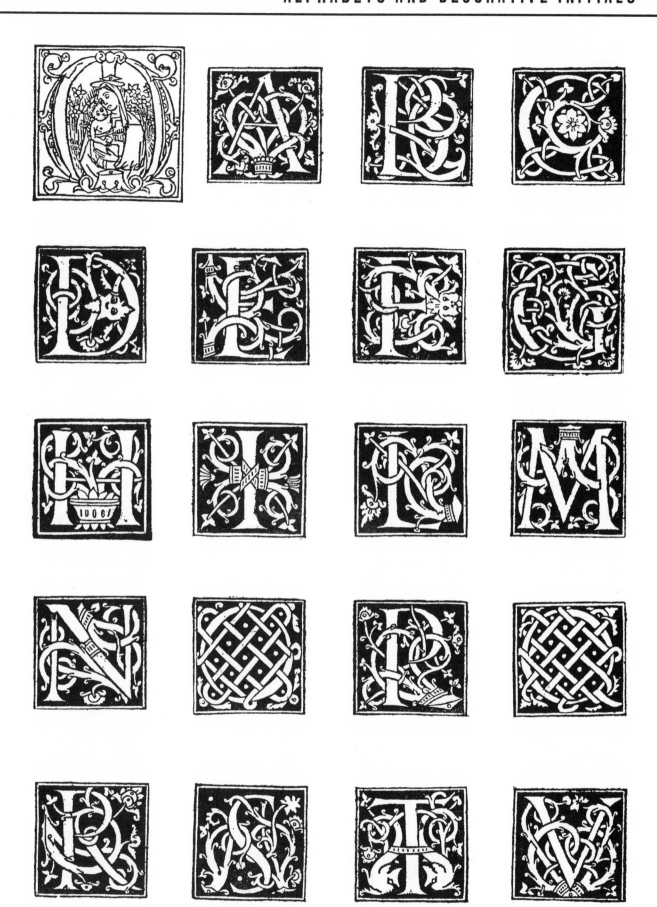

The printing center of Lyons used initials like these—first quarter
of the 16th century

A simple and charming set of Venetian initials—Philippus Pincius, 1504

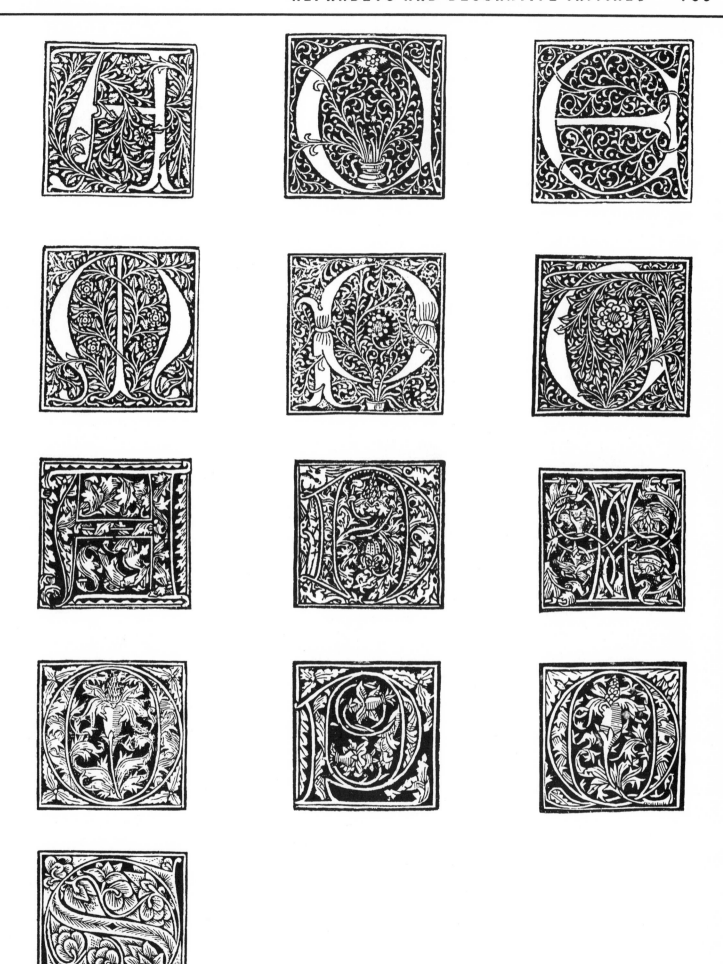

The early German printers in Spain used initials such as these, 1492-1497

Initials in criblé manner, possibly cut in metal—André Bocard, Paris, 1491-1531

A kind of initial often used in the late 15th century—these at Lyons

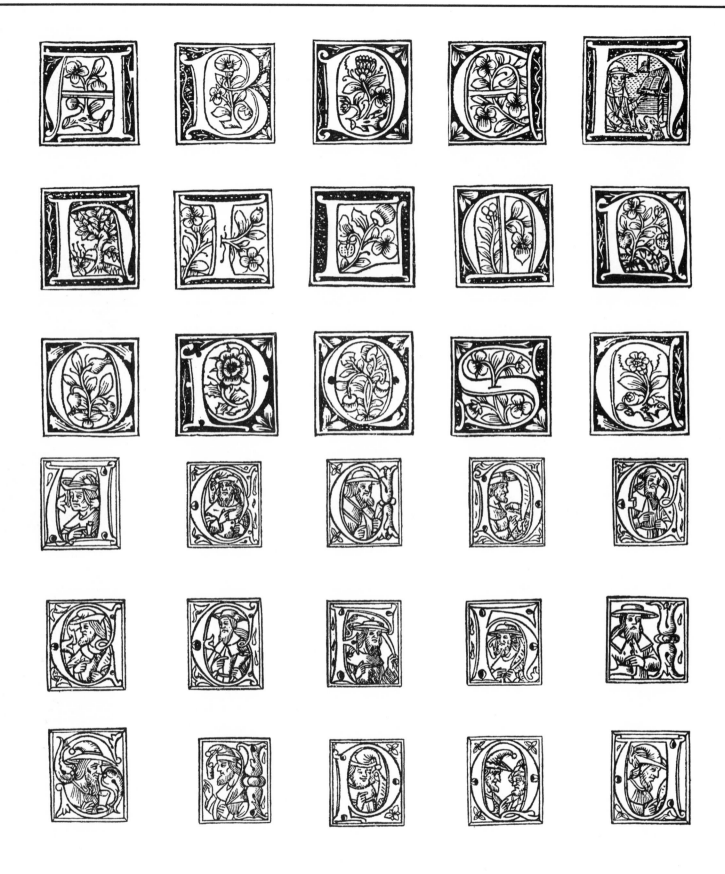

Initials from the Ferrara-Florence area, apparently used by various printers, 1497

Birds, beasts, and flowers—used by Jacques Sacon, Lyons, 1519

Jacob Köbel's initials, 1518—Italian influence on German printers

Cherubs and children by Anton Woensam, used at Cologne, first half of the 16th century

The female form and the vagaries of love—from the Egenolff press, Frankfurt, 1543

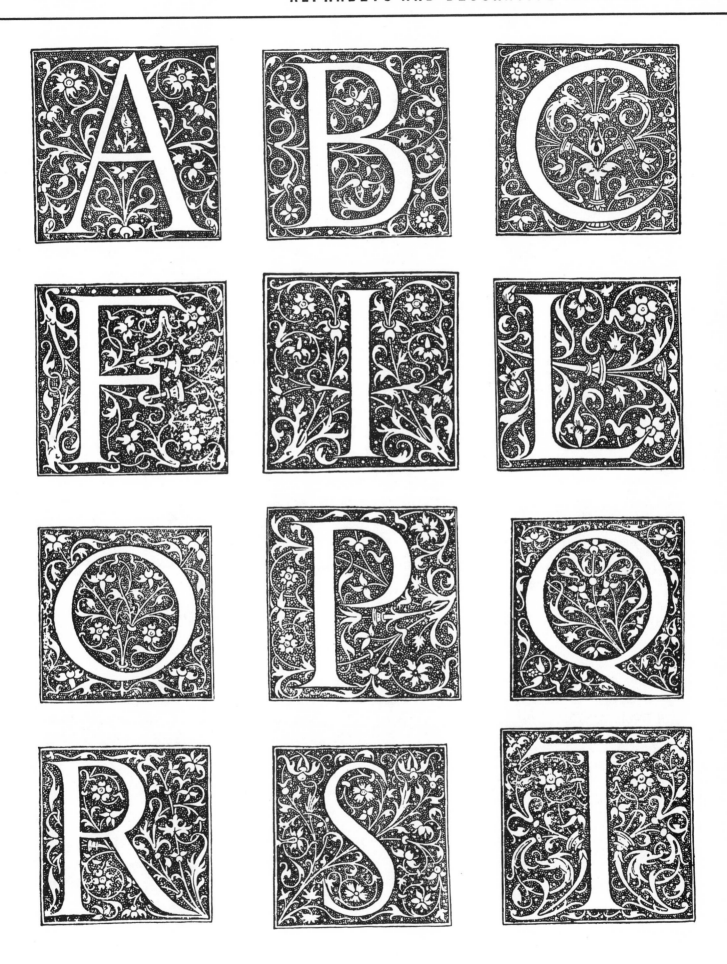

Geoffroy Tory's fame rests largely on these lovely initials—Paris, 1522-1529

Oronce Finé, the mathematician, designed these initials in Paris, 1532

A set of thistle initials used by the printer Denys Janot, 1544

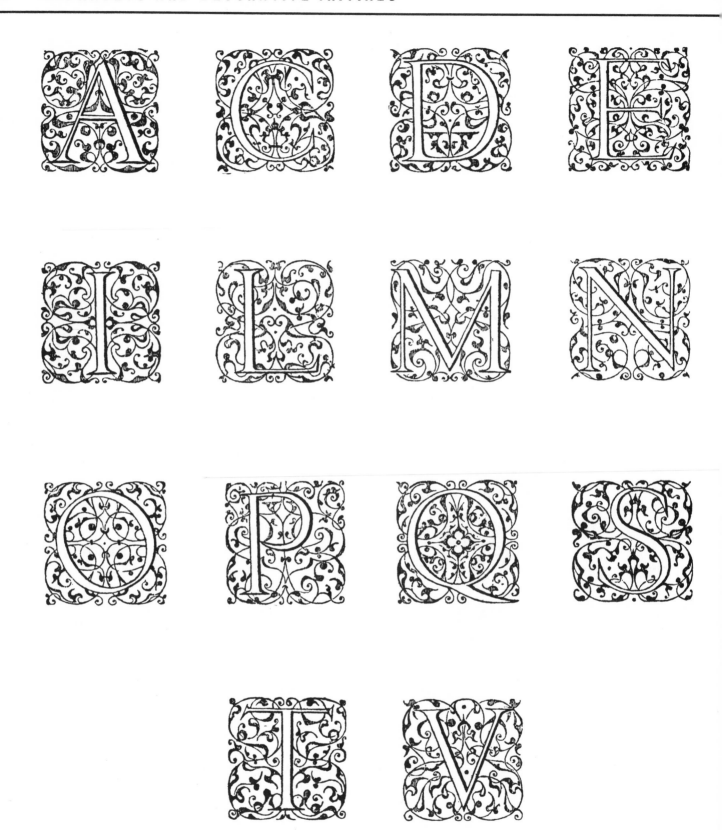

Arabesques like these were popular after 1550—used by
Jean Crespin at Geneva

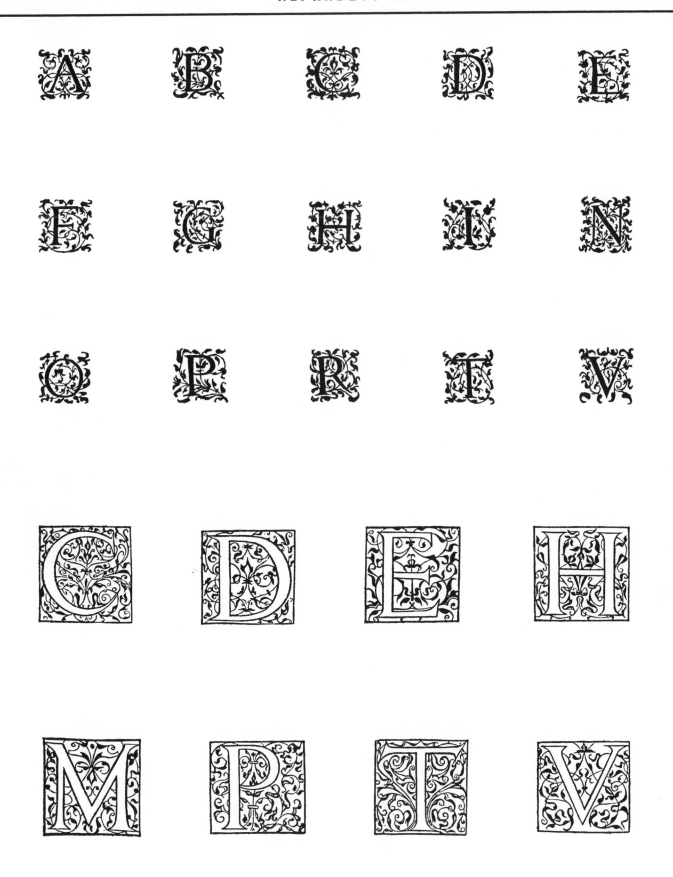

Two sets of French initials in the arabesque manner—
later part of the 16th century

These initials are related to those used by Plantin and by Adam Berg

This sort of initial was used in music books about 1600

Dutch initials of the 17th century—the basket-of-flowers was a
much-used design

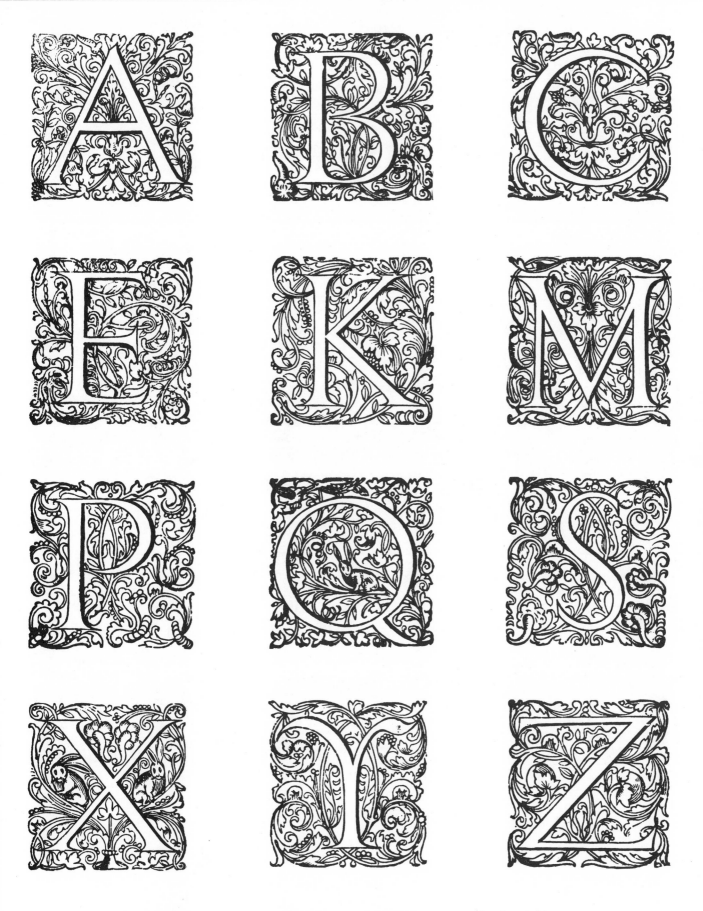

The blocks of these 17th-century initials still exist at the firm of
Enschedé, Haarlem

Initials were also produced by copperplate engraving—these are Dutch, late 1600's

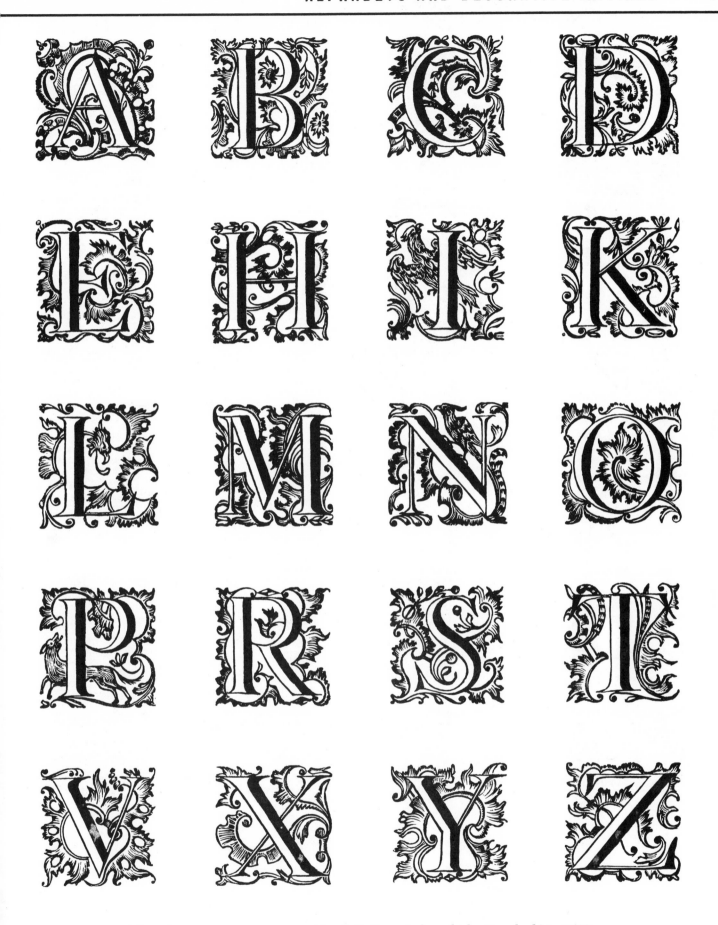

These letters were cut on metal by J. F. Rosart—bought by Enschedé in 1760

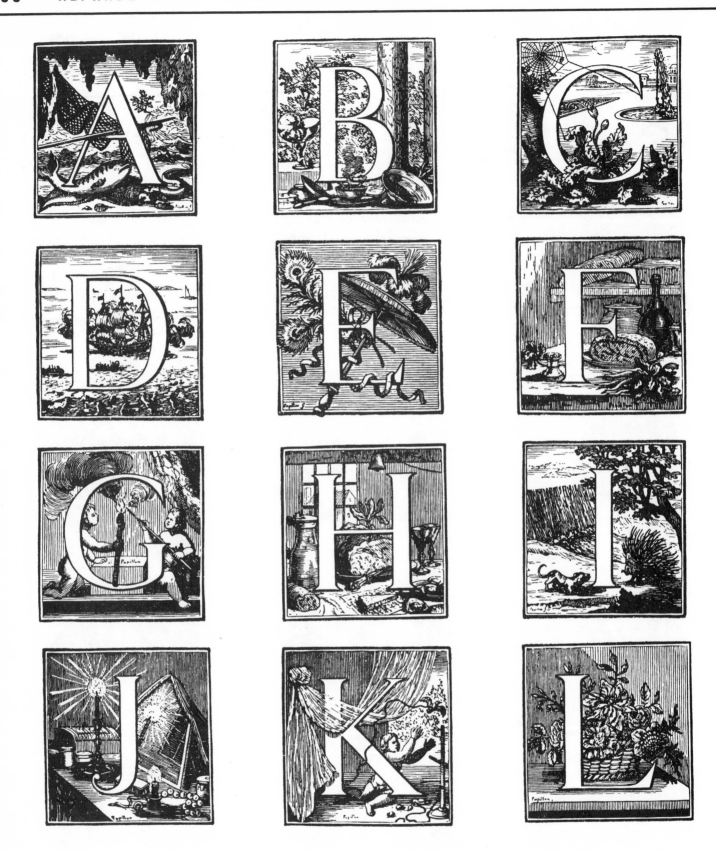

Woodcut initials by Jean Michel Papillon—first shown in Paris, 1760

Jean Michel was a son of Jean Papillon, the famous manufacturer
of fine wallpapers

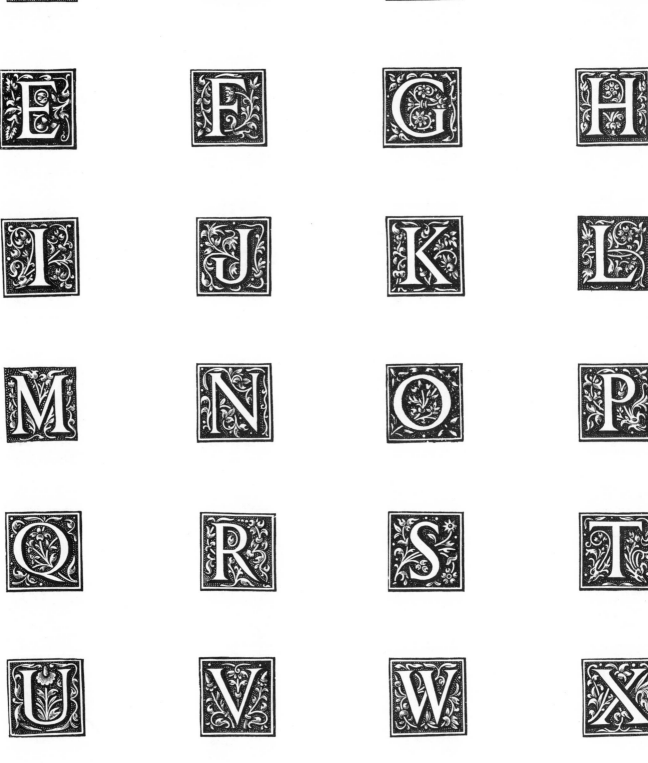

A revival design—used by the Chiswick Press in England,
middle of the 19th century

A rather original alphabet used by the Chiswick Press—
based on Gothic initials

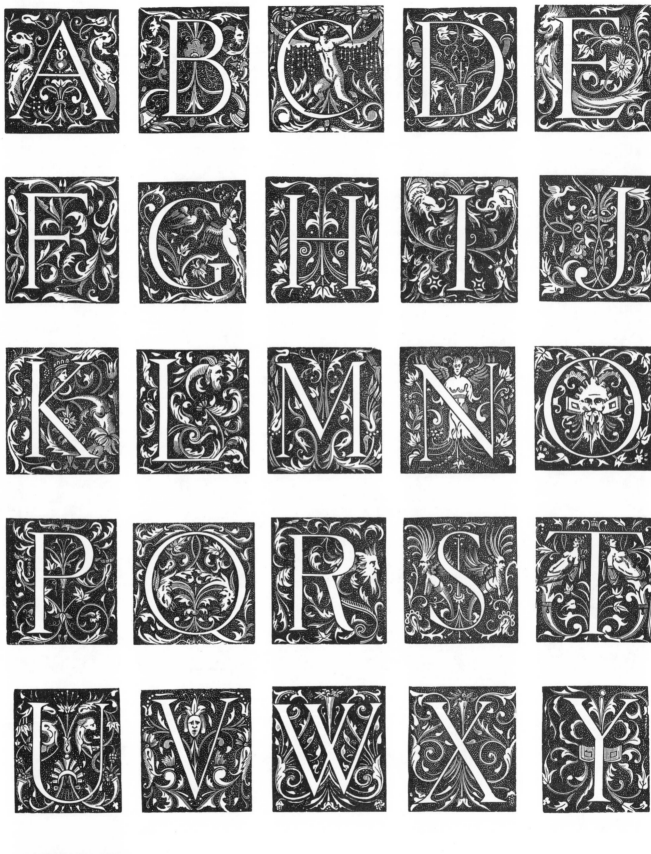

A set of initials used in England about 1880—possibly of
French origin, cut in wood

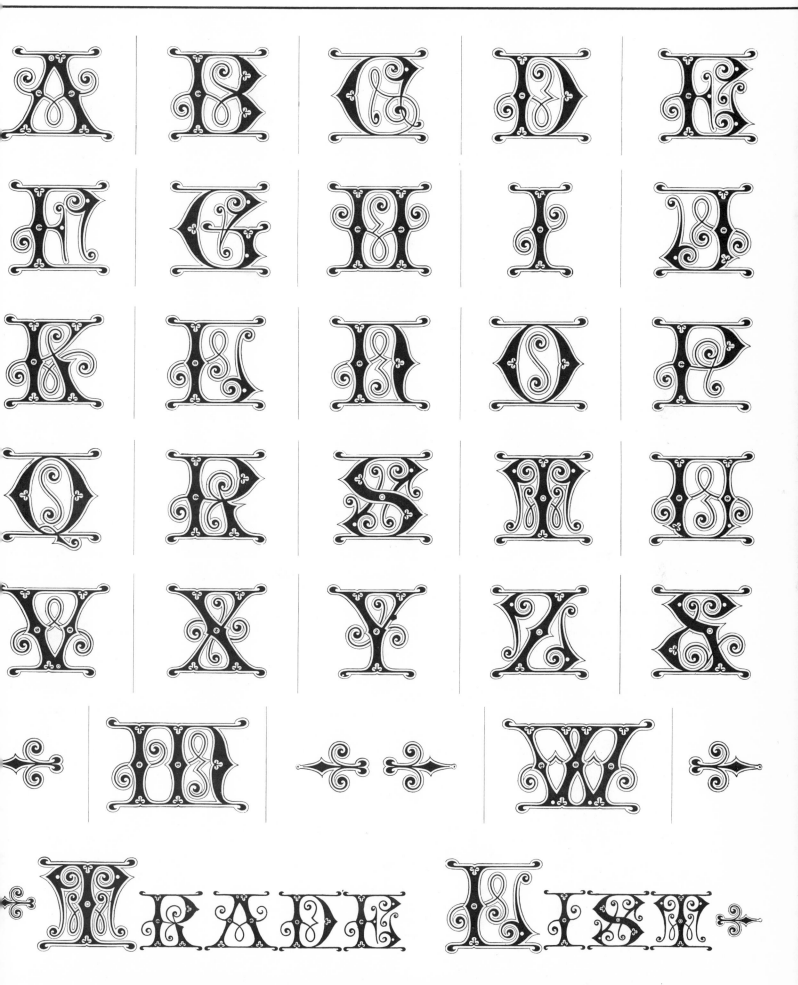

These initials were called Medieval, but they are really Victorian gingerbread, 1890

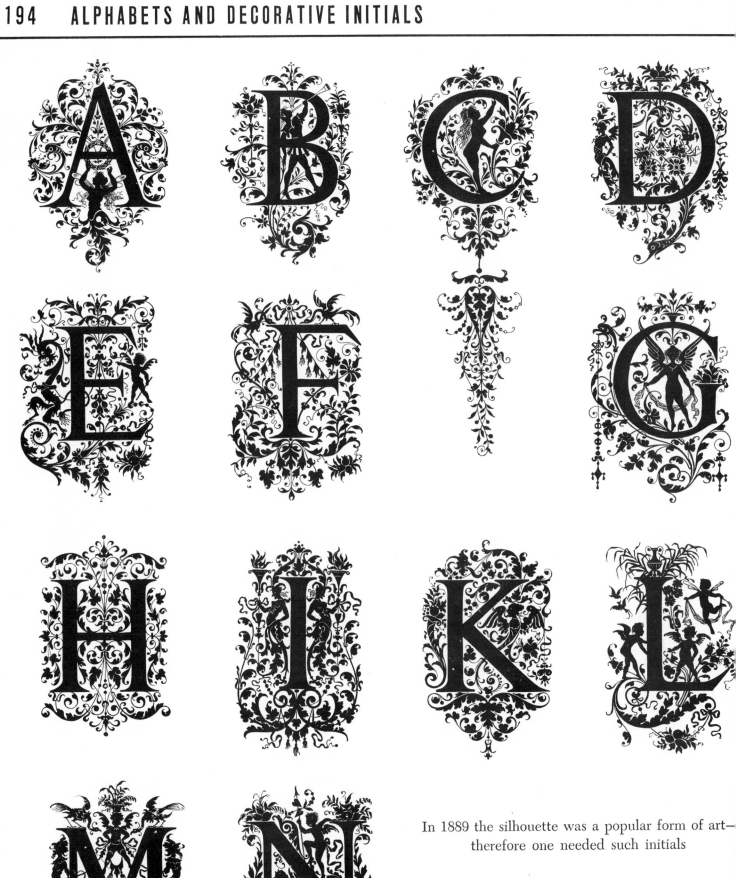

In 1889 the silhouette was a popular form of art—
therefore one needed such initials

More silhouette initials—they are essentially a variety of the arabesque

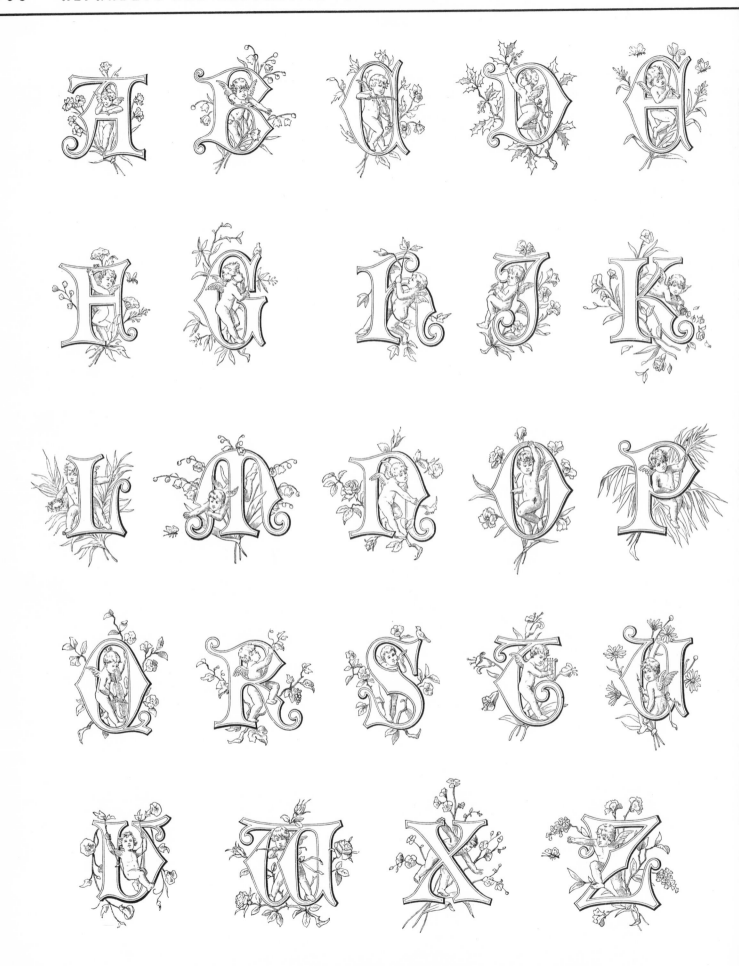

Gothic initials with superimposed sentimentality—called Amorette,
and used about 1889

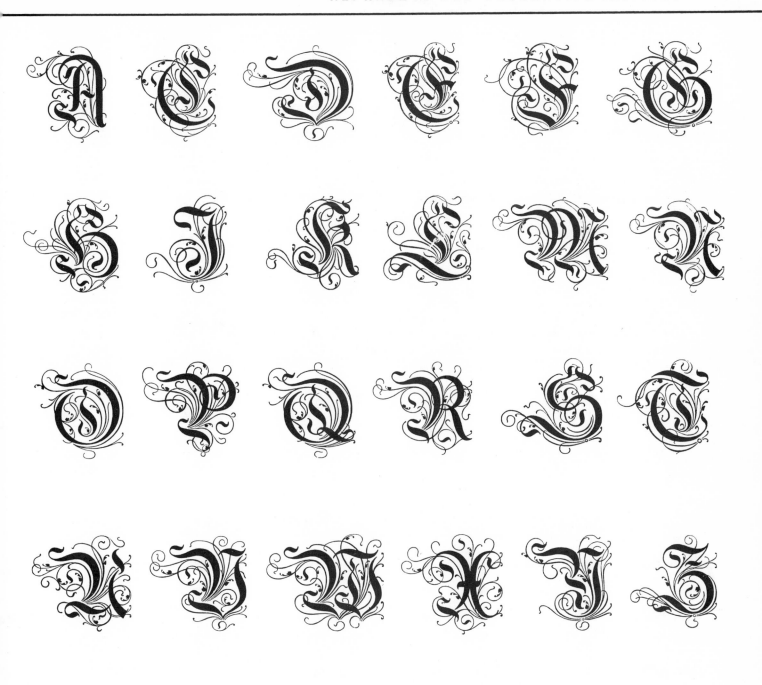

Revival of a Gothic chancery letter—related to the Fraktur design—
German 1880's

Tuscan.

A B C D E F G H I J K L M N

O P Q R S T U V W X Y Z &

a b c d e f g h i j k l m n o p q r

1 2 3 4 5 s t u v w x y z 6 7 8 9 0.

F. S. Copley. Del.

Italian Print

A B C D E F G H I J K L M

N O P Q R S T U V W X Y Z

a b c d e f g h i j k l m n o p q r s

1 2 3 4 5 t u v w x y z 6 7 8 9 0

Two basic 19th-century styles—Tuscan, with forked ends, and Italian

ROMAN PRINT, VARIOUSLY SHADED.

A B C D E F G H I
J K L M N O P Q R
S T U V W X Y Z &

ITALIC PRINT, VARIOUSLY SHADED.

A B C D E F G H I J K L M
N O P Q R S T U V W X Y Z

a b c d e f g h i j k l m n o p q r s t u v w x y z.

Here are a few of the shading ideas used by 19th-century lithographers and engravers

Gothic revival of the 1880's, with non-Gothic doodling as a
background—German

Alt-Deutſch.

Holländiſch-Gotiſch.

Verzierte Alt-Gotiſch.

Verzierte Gotiſch.

Nineteenth-century varieties of Dutch, German, and decorated Gothics

Favorit.

Phantasie.

Here are two Gothic alphabets with typical 19th-century aberrations and trimmings

Scroll Alphabet

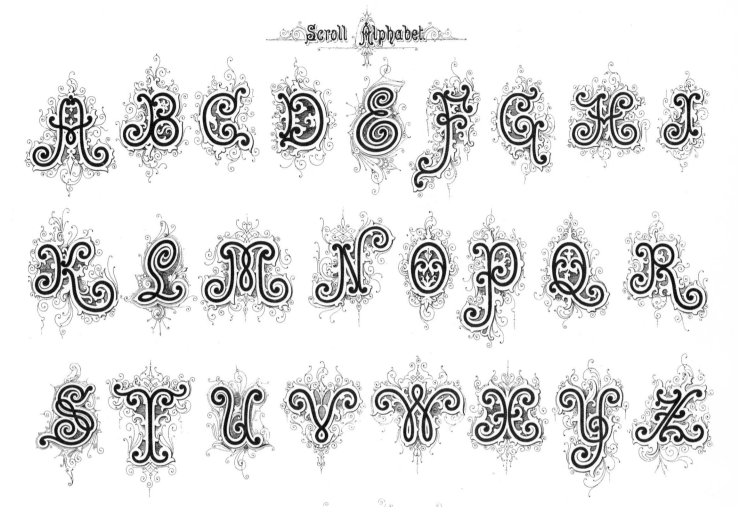

Rustic Alphabet

Shrubbery of all kinds was used for initials during the last part of the 19th century

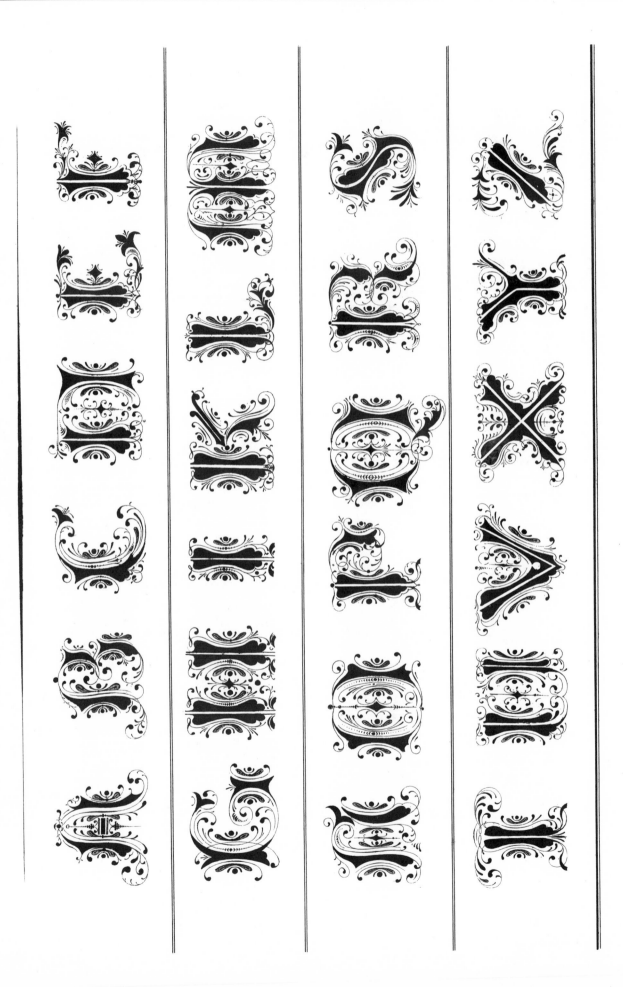

ROMAINE MIDOLLINE.

A 19th-century alphabet derived from an Italian 16th-century style

ALPHABET LAPIDAIRE MONSTRE.

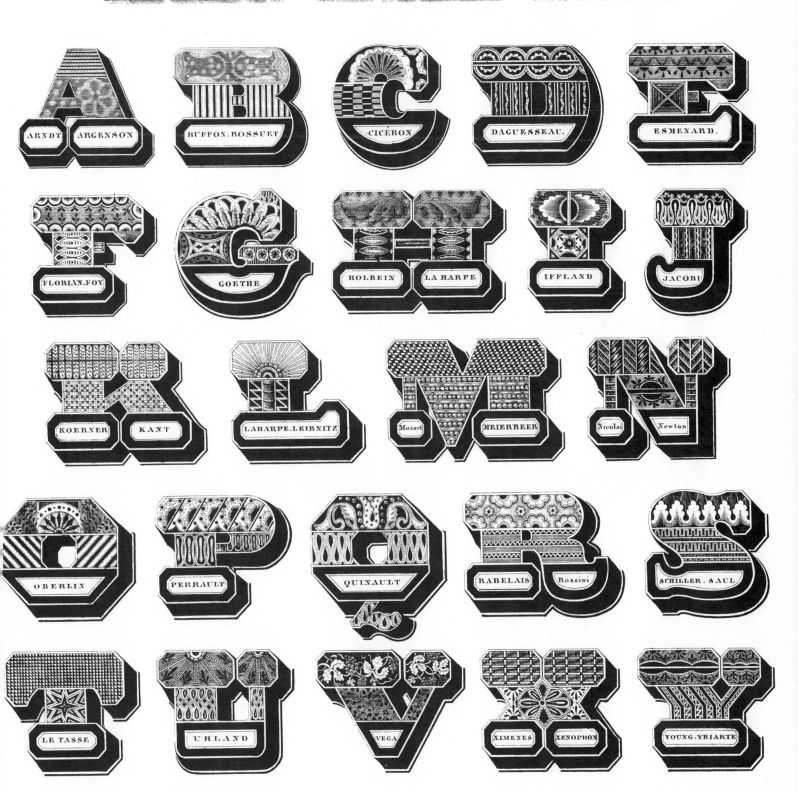

This 19th-century alphabet was called Lapidaire Monstre—
which it is, to say the least

Rather fine late 19th-century revival of Florentine Renaissance
initials—German

Second half of the Florentine alphabet—color and texture are uneven
(note the S)

Schmale Jonisch.

ABCDEF
GHIJKLMN
OPQRSTUV
WXYZ

Schattierte Jonisch.

ABCDEFGHI
JKLMNOPQRST
UVWXYZ
abcdefghijklmno
pqrstuvwxyz
1234567890

Halbfette Egyptienne.

ABCDEFGHIJ
KLMNOPQRSTU
VWXYZ
abcdefghijklmno
pqrstuvwxyz

Breite Egyptienne.

ABCDEFGHIJKLMNO
PQRSTUVWXYZ
abcdefghijklmnopqrstu
vwwxyz 67890
ABCDEFGHIJKLMN O
PQRSTUVWXYZ
abcdefghijklmnopqrstu
1 2 3 4 5 vwwxyz 6 7 8 9 0

Lichte Jonisch.

ABCDE
FGHIJK
LMOP
QRSTUV
WXYZ

Kursiv.

ABCDEFGHI
JKLMNOPQRS
TUVWXYZ
abcdefghijklmn
opqrstuvwxyz
1234567890

Another basic 19th-century style: Egyptian, sometimes Ionic, better called Square Serif

Clarendon.

ABCDEFGHIJKLMNOPQRS
12345 TUVWXYZ 67890
abcdefghijklmnopqrstuvwxyz

Richard BREMEN Wagner

Schriftgiesserei von Bauer & Comp. in Stuttgart.

Breite verzierte Clarendon.

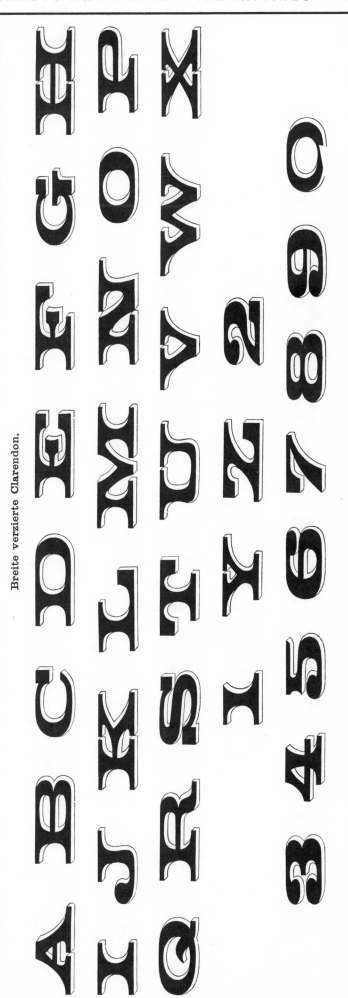

The Clarendons were also developed in the 19th century–also a basic style

Breite (geschweifte) Italienne.

Italienne Kursiv (verziert).

Schriftgiesserei von Genzsch & Heyse in Hamburg.

Schattierte Italienne.

Italienne.

Schriftgiesserei von Genzsch & Heyse in Hamburg.

Italienne Kursiv.

Schriftgiesserei von Julius Klinkhardt in Leipzig.

Schriftgiesserei Flinsch in Frankfurt a. M.

Breite Italienne.

Schriftgiesserei von Schelter & Giesecke in Leipzig.

Italian is distinguished by wrong-way weights—there is little reason for the name

These initials cost 60¢ apiece in 1890—with special filigree border $1.00

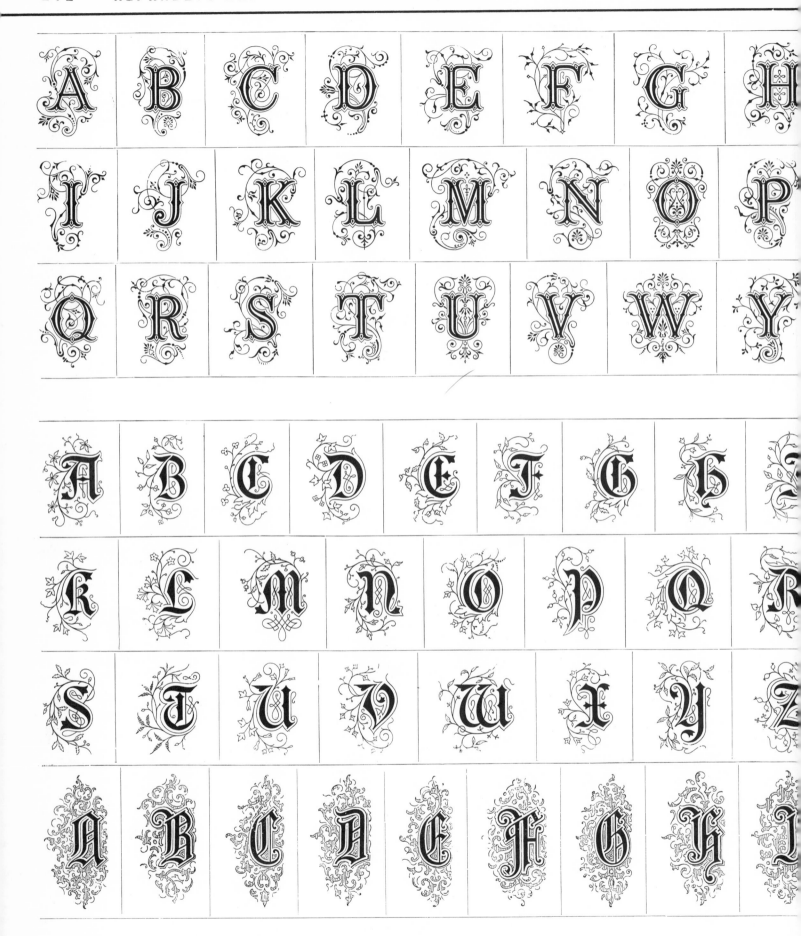

Arabesque designs appeared again in the 19th century—
some were rather pretty

Gothic-revival initials based on the 14th-century "closed letter"
design—1890

English revival of the arabesque design dating from about 1900

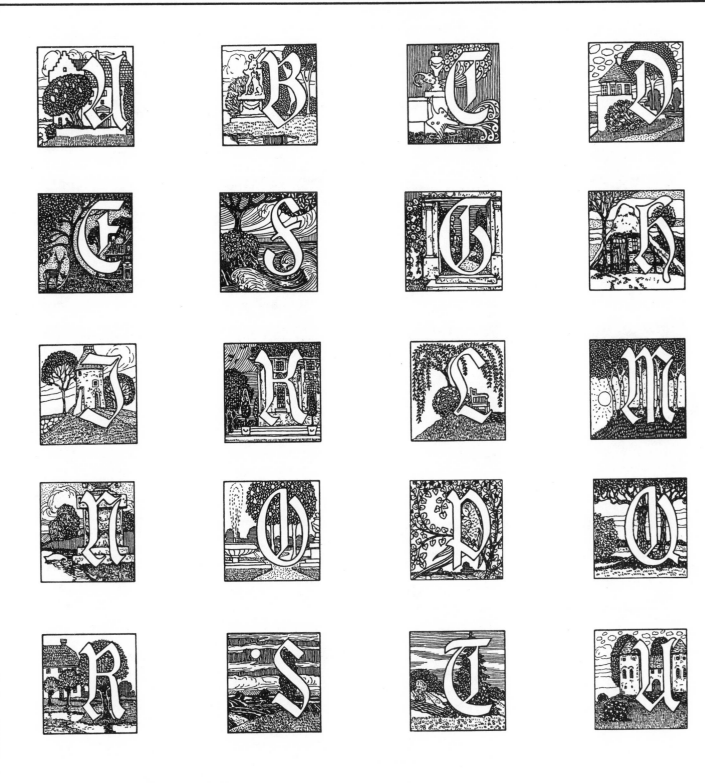

A Jugendstil alphabet produced in Germany in the early 1900's

A set of wood-engraved initials—the terrors of night life—
Riga, Latvia, 1924

HORNET.

WAYNE.

RICHES

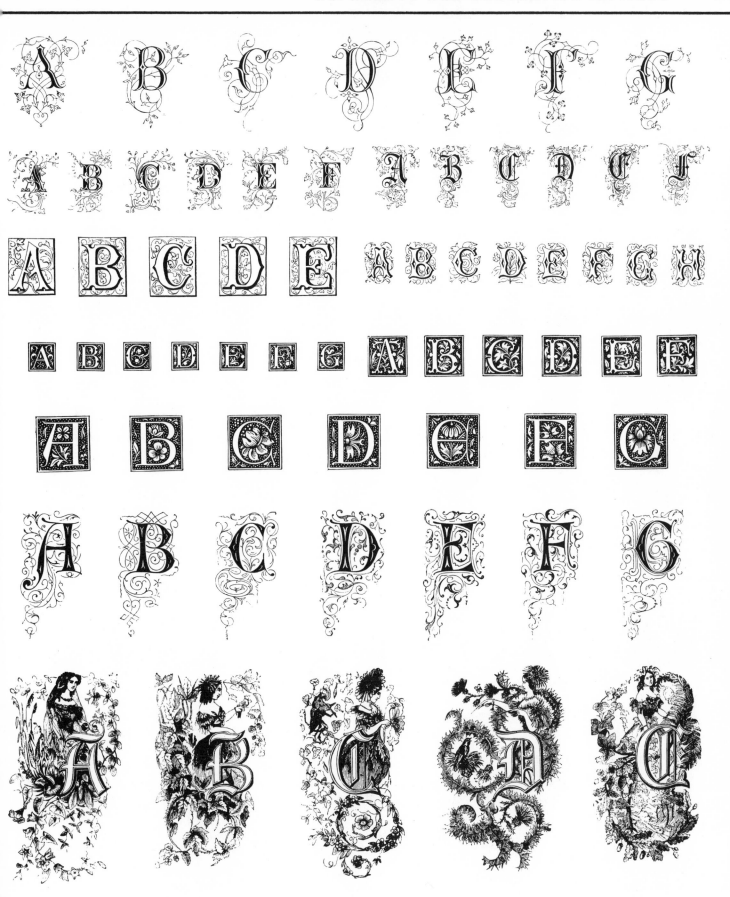

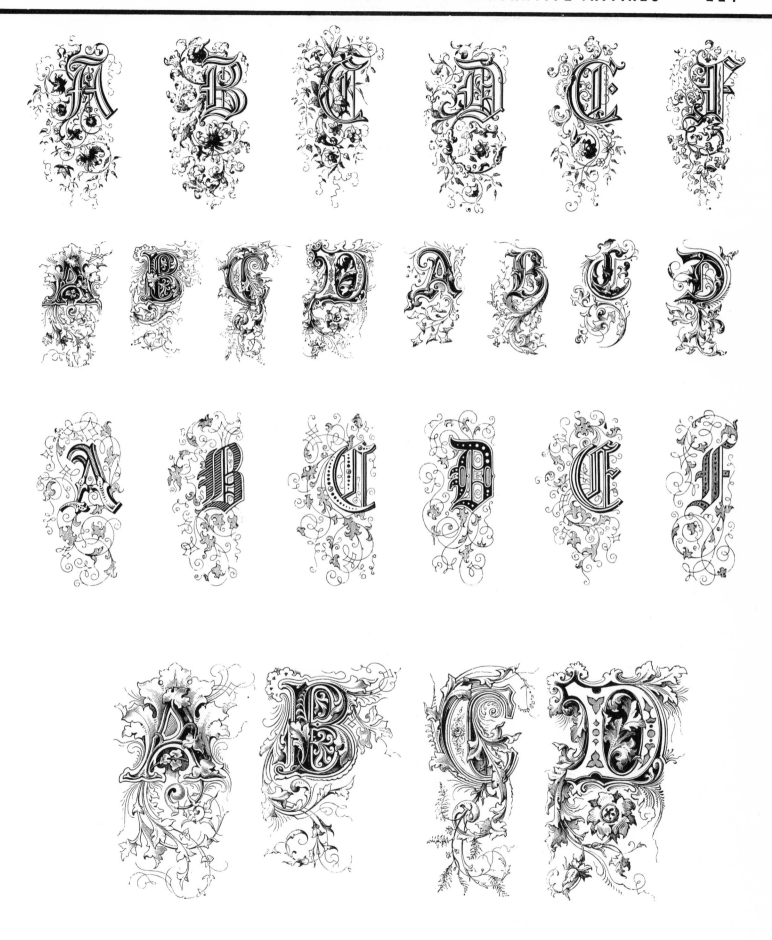

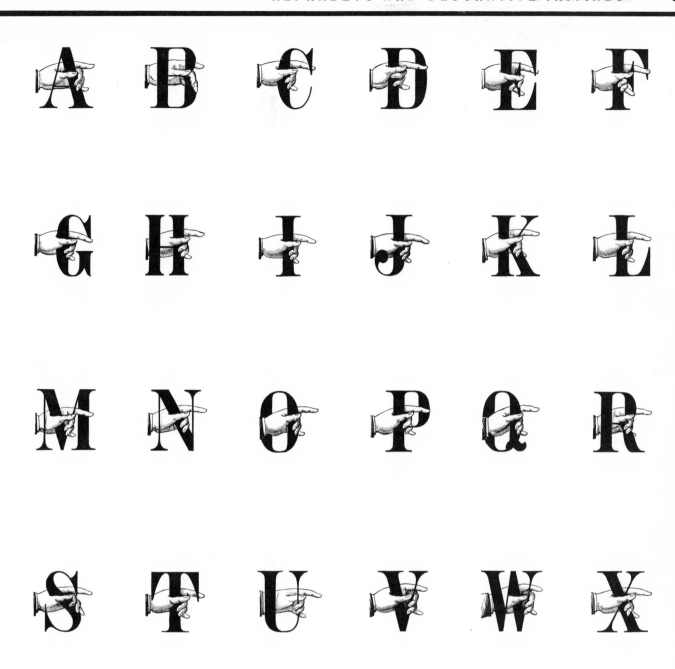

WE POINT with pride to the productions of the
BRAINCRAFT AND HANDICRAFT
of those connected with this establishment
during the century which is now approaching its close

BILLHEAD LOGOTYPES.

Office of *Office of* **Office** OF *Office* OF *Office*

Bought of **BOUGHT OF** **OFFICE OF** *Bought of* **BOUGHT** OF

Bought of **BOUGHT** OF **BOUGHT** OF *Bought of*

BOUGHT OF *Bought of* **BOUGHT** OF *Bought of*

Bought of **Received** **Bought of**

Bought of  **Bought of**

Bought of  *Bought of*

Bought of **Received** *Bought of*

Bought of **Received** *Bought of*

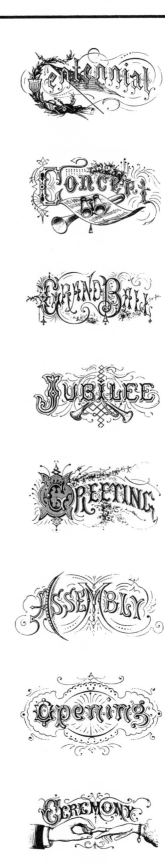

Ornamental Flourishes.

ORNAMENTAL FLOURISHES.

ORNAMENTAL FLOURISHES.

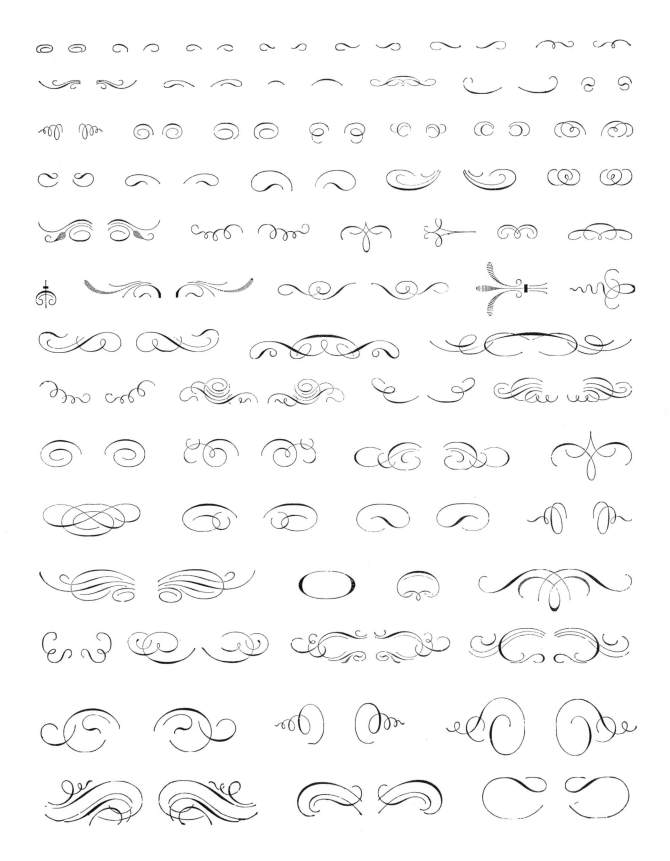

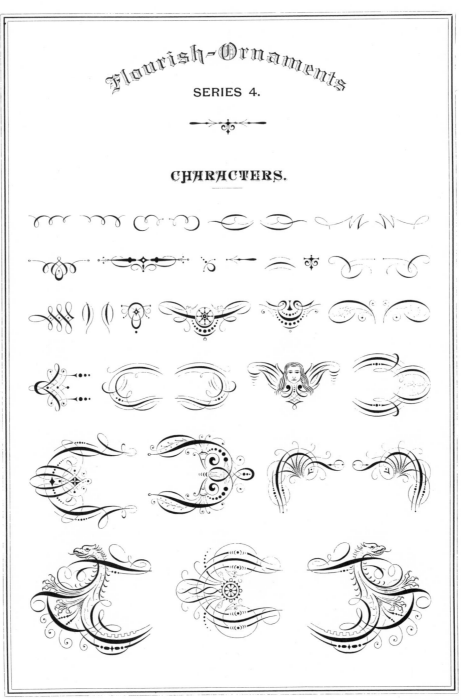

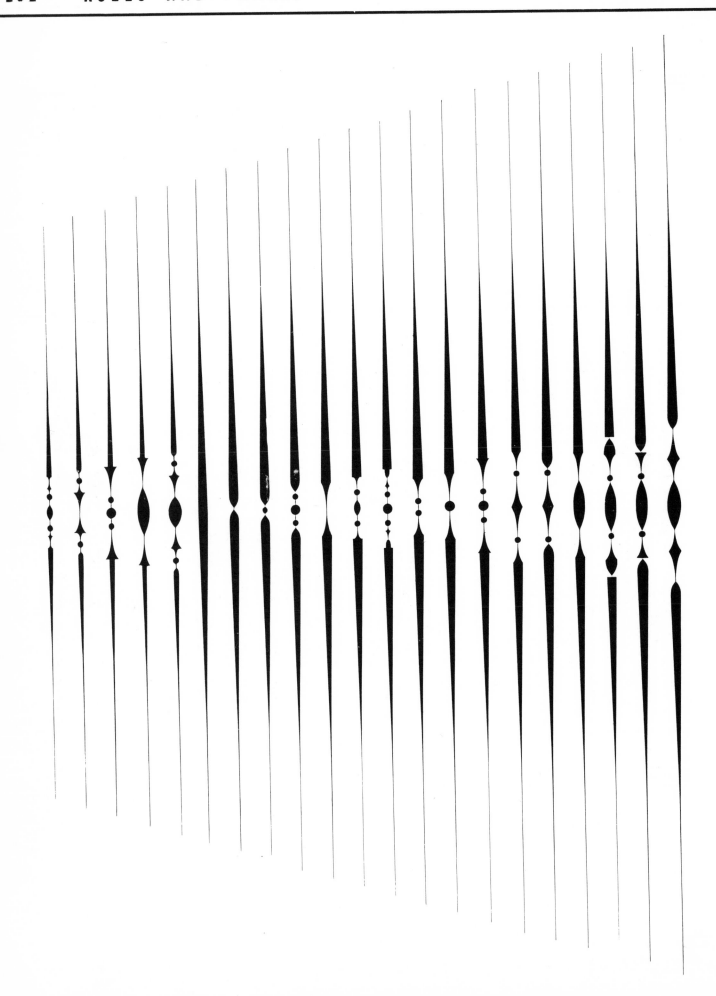

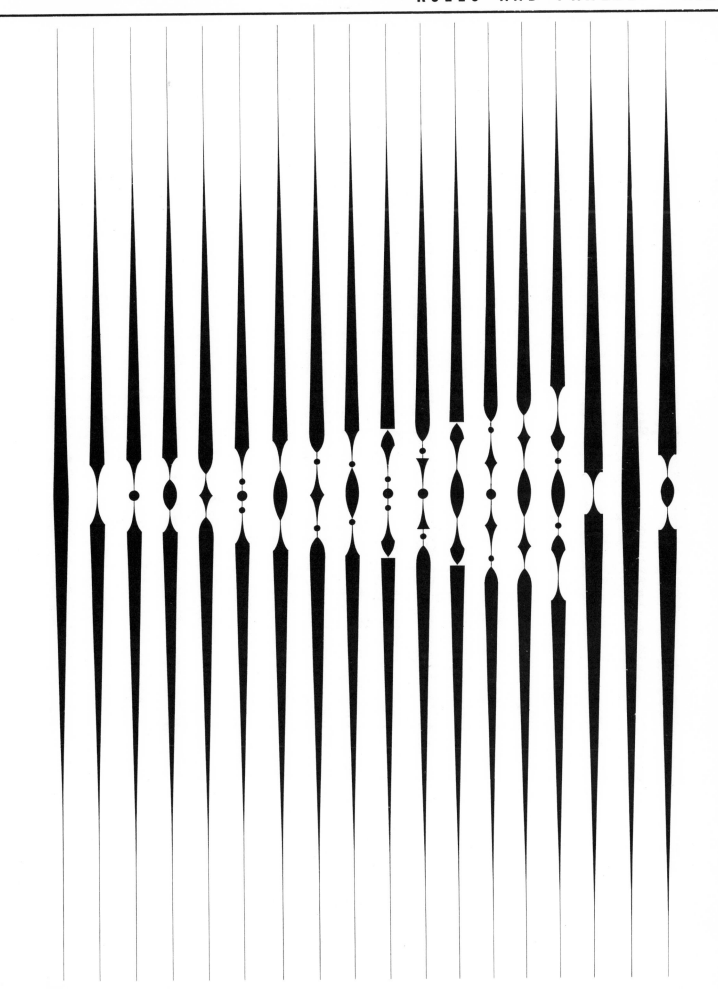

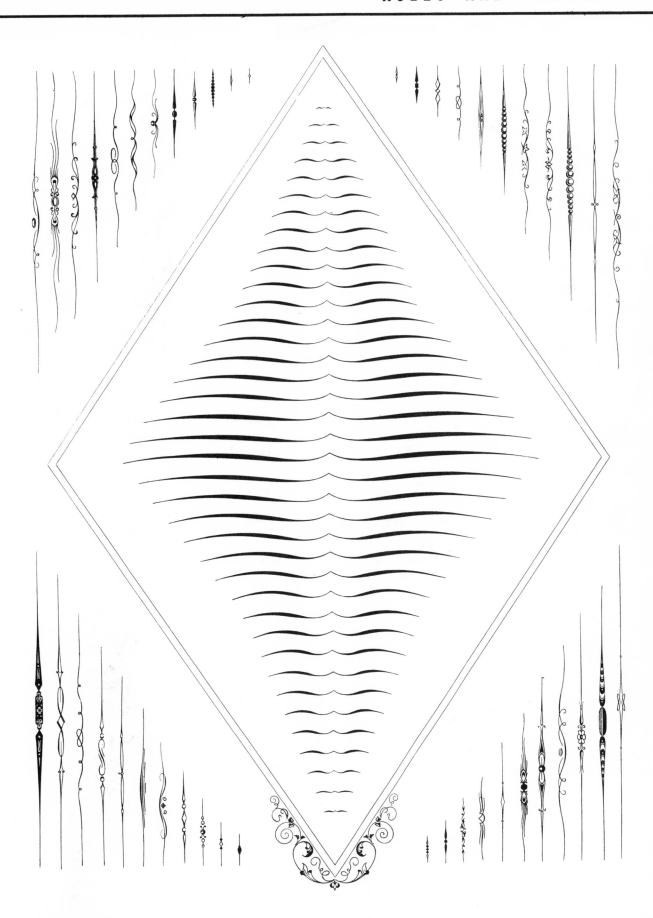

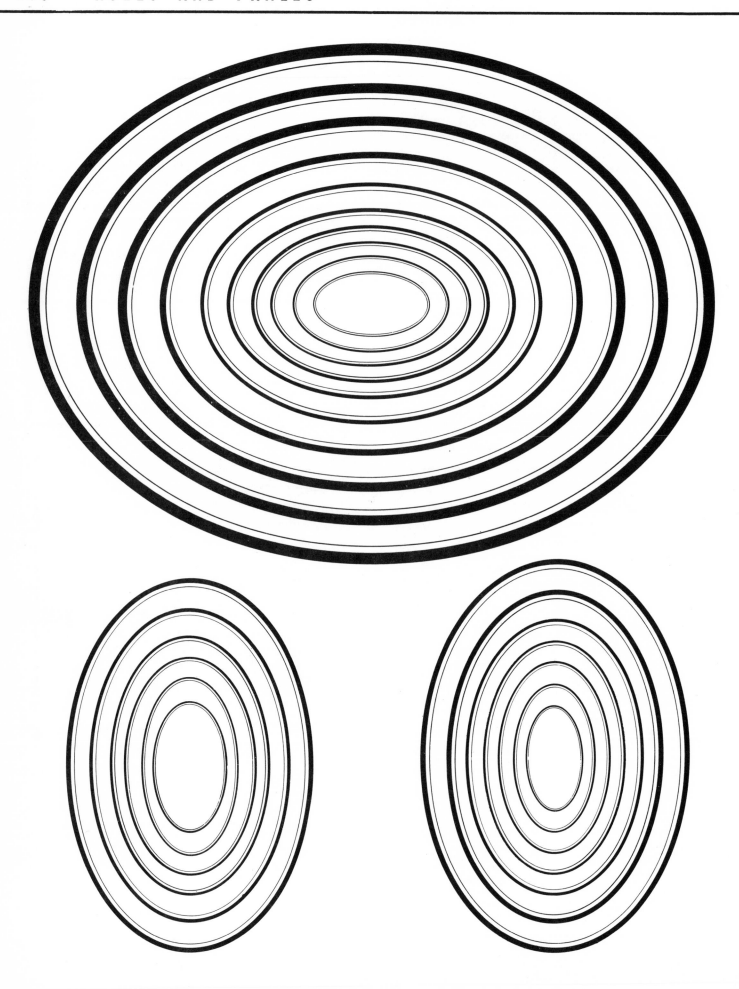

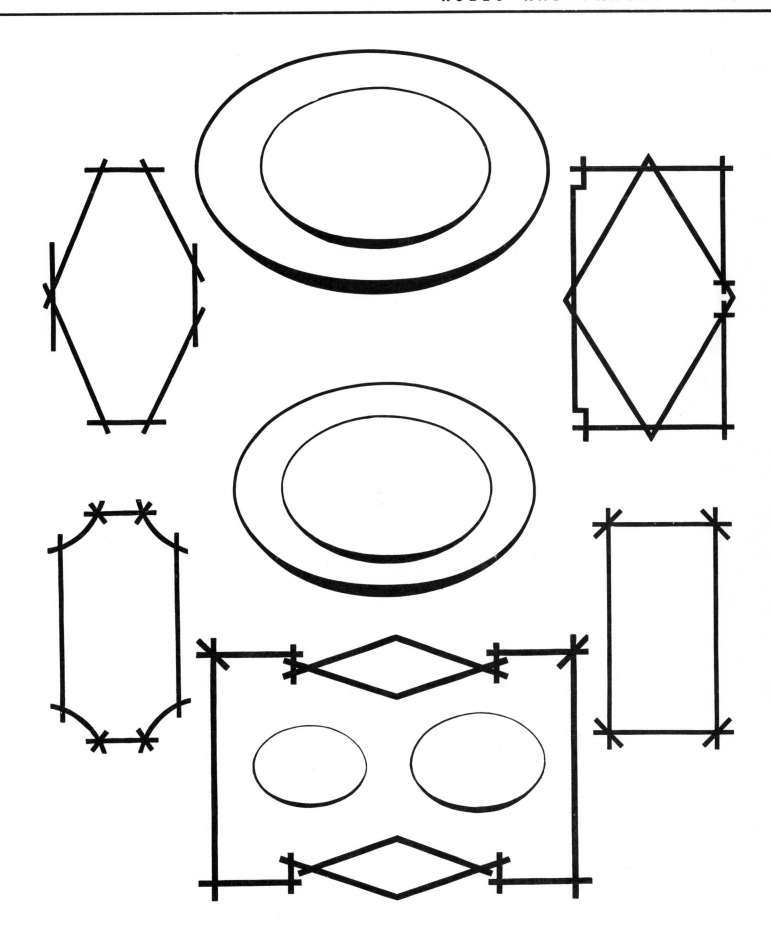

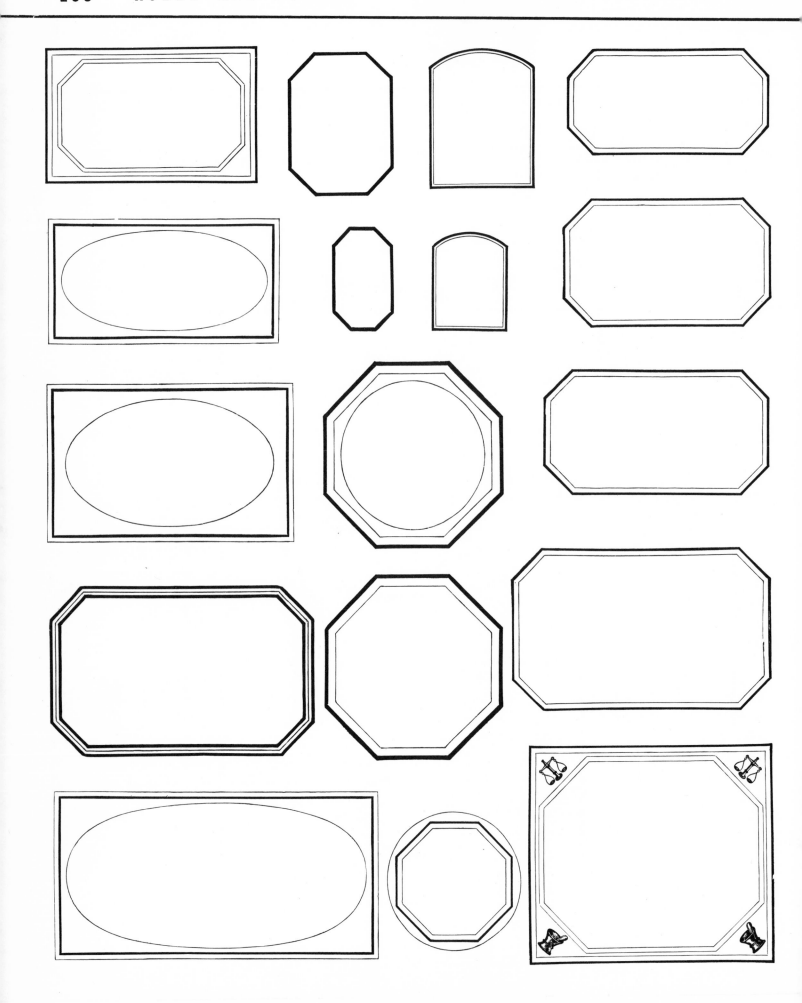

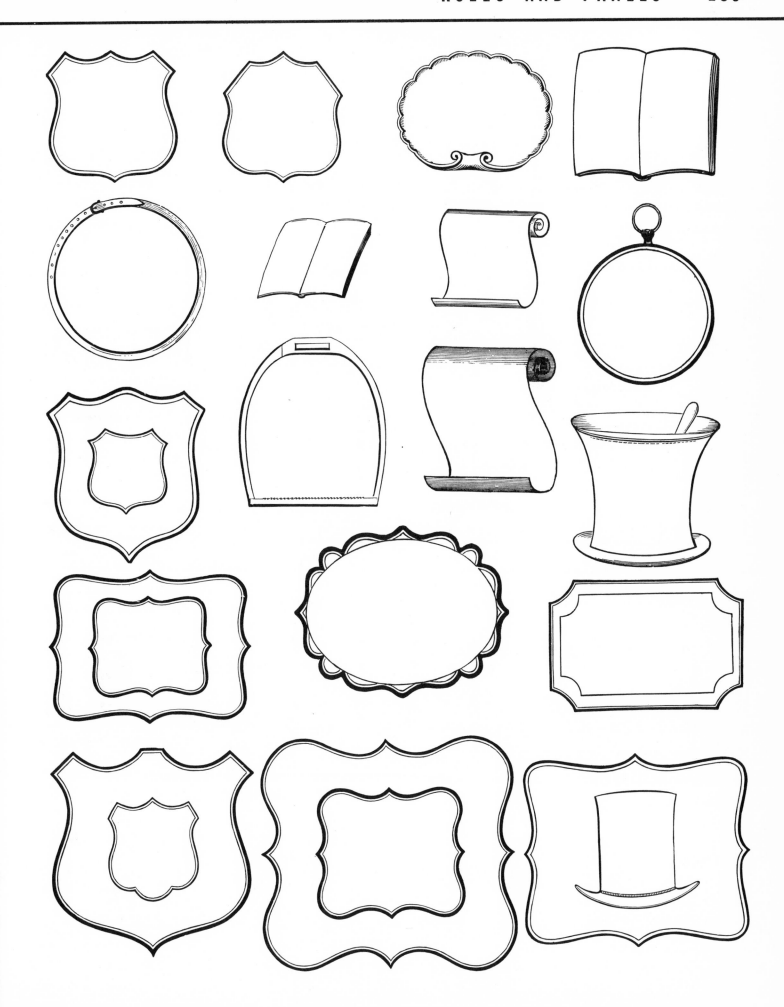

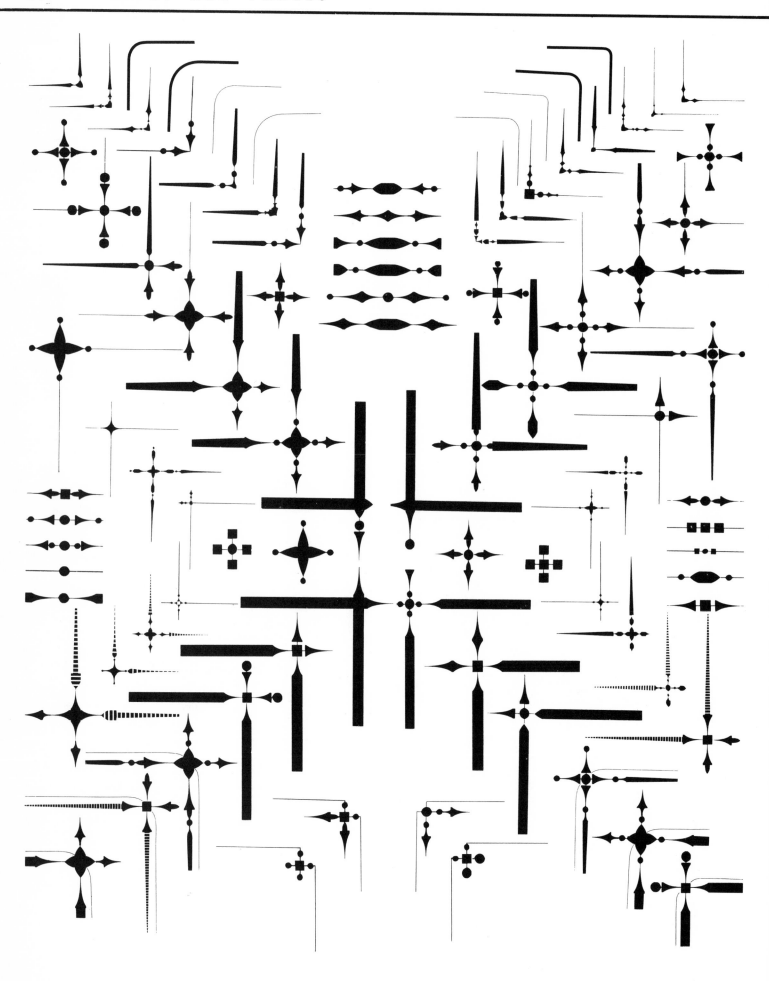

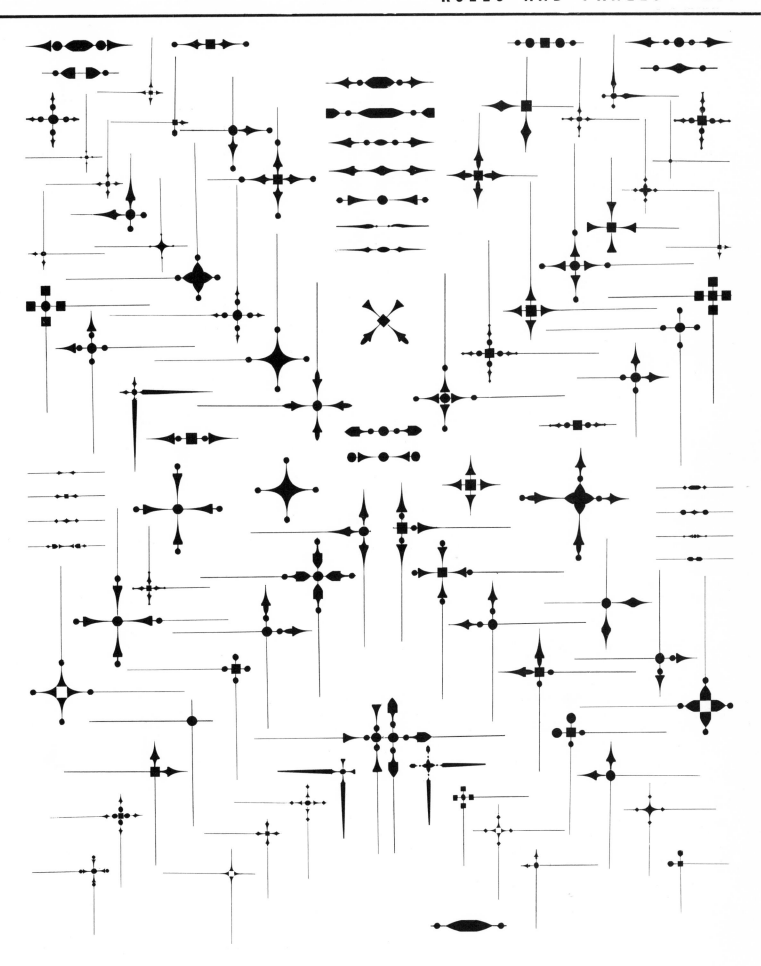

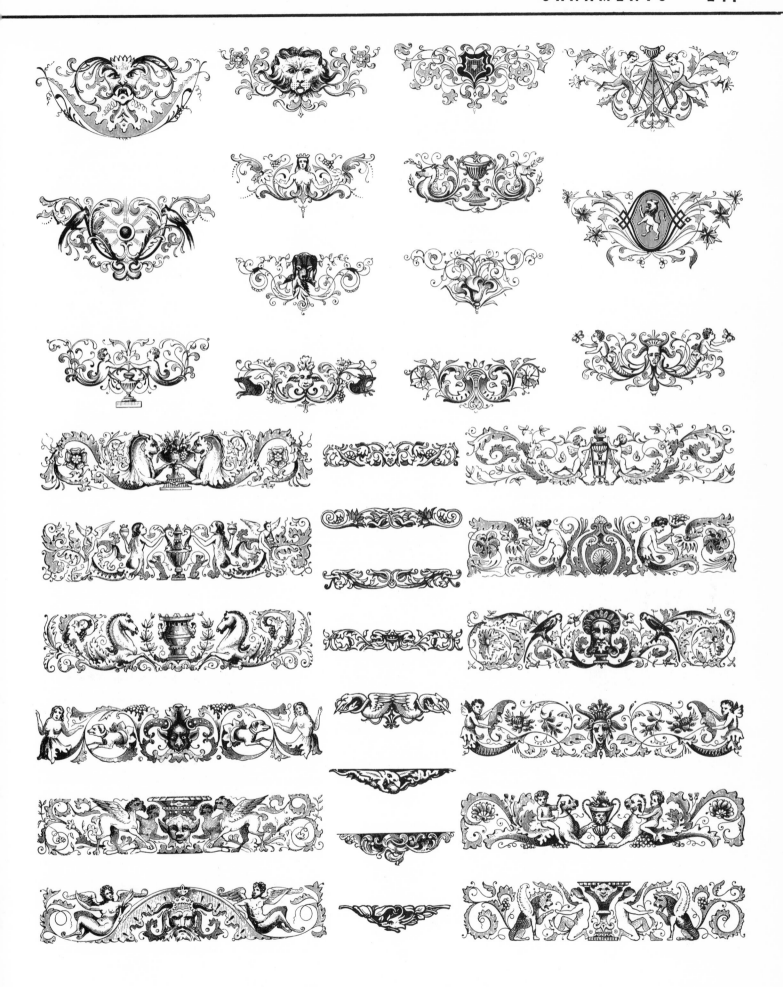

EGYPTIAN BORDER

SOLOMON FERNWOOD & CO.

PAPER PULP AND MUMMY PHOSPHATES,

CAIRO, EGYPT.

MOSES & LEVY,

DEALERS IN MINIATURE PYRAMIDS,

ALEXANDRIA.

SAND-STREWN PYRAMIDS AND

GRAVE SCENES IN PHARAOHLAND.

Banks.

COSMOPOLITAN TOURISTS ASCENDING THE NILE.

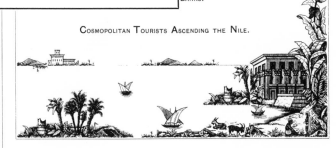

Vintage of the Year 1796

National Holiday

Betrothal

SAINT VALENTINE'S FESTIVAL

Mortised Ornaments

CHARACTERS.

Indenture

FOR REAL ESTATE PURCHASE

Soiree

WITH PANORAMIC VIEWS

Catalogue

OF DELINQUENT MEMBERS

Section

ON THE SOUTHWEST CORNER

Conclusion

Chapter 1.

Iron=Bound Buckets

FOR LAWN DECORATIONS

CEREMONY
THURSDAY   MORNING.

BRIDAL   WREATHS.

KNIGHTS TEMPLAR
IN THIS SIGN   WE CONQUER

CHURCH OF   CEREMONY   ST. SWITHIN

GRAND   I. O. of O. F.   UNION.

MASONIC
SOCIAL   CIRCLE.

THURSDAY   EVENING
RECEPTION.

MASONIC   TEMPLE
FESTIVAL.

ENCAMPMENT
AMERICAN   MECHANICS

REDMEN'S
ANNUAL   COUNCIL.

AMERICAN MECHANICS'
NOBLE   GUILD.

LO! THE POOR INDIAN.
REDMEN'S   POWWOW.

KNIGHTS   HONOUR   TEMPLAR.

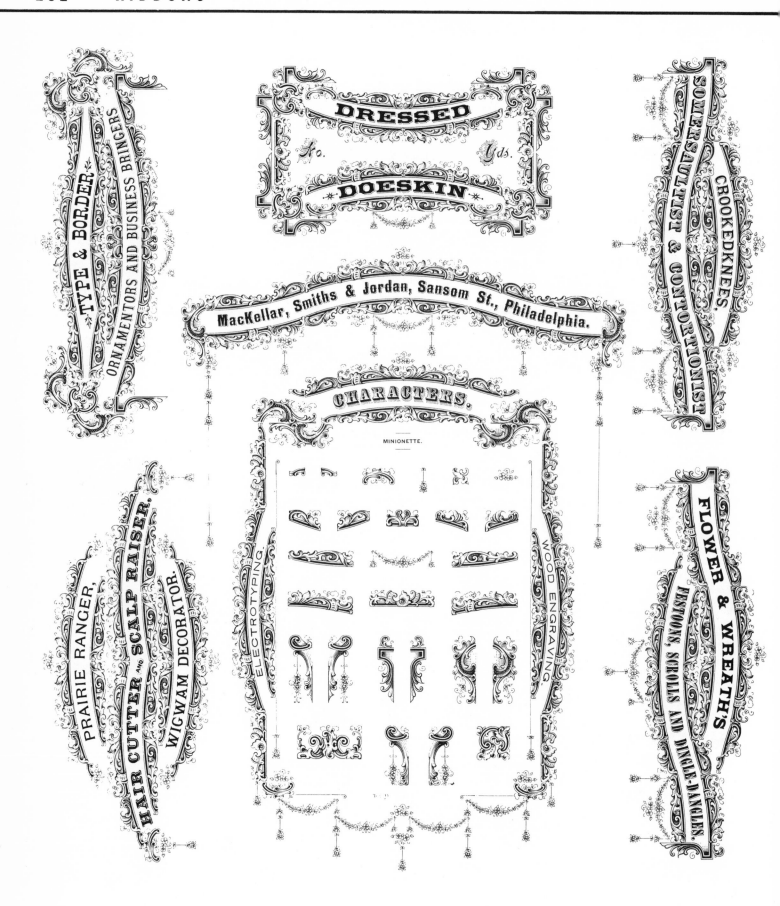

TYPE & BORDER.

ORNAMENTORS AND BUSINESS BRINGERS.

DRESSED

No.

Yds.

DOESKIN

SOMERSAULTIST & CONTORTIONIST

CROOKEDKNEES.

MacKellar, Smiths & Jordan, Sansom St., Philadelphia.

CHARACTERS.

MINIONETTE.

PRAIRIE RANGER,

HAIR CUTTER and SCALP RAISER,

WIGWAM DECORATOR.

ELECTROTYPING.

WOOD ENGRAVING.

FLOWER & WREATH'S

FESTOONS, SCROLLS AND DINGLE-DANGLES.

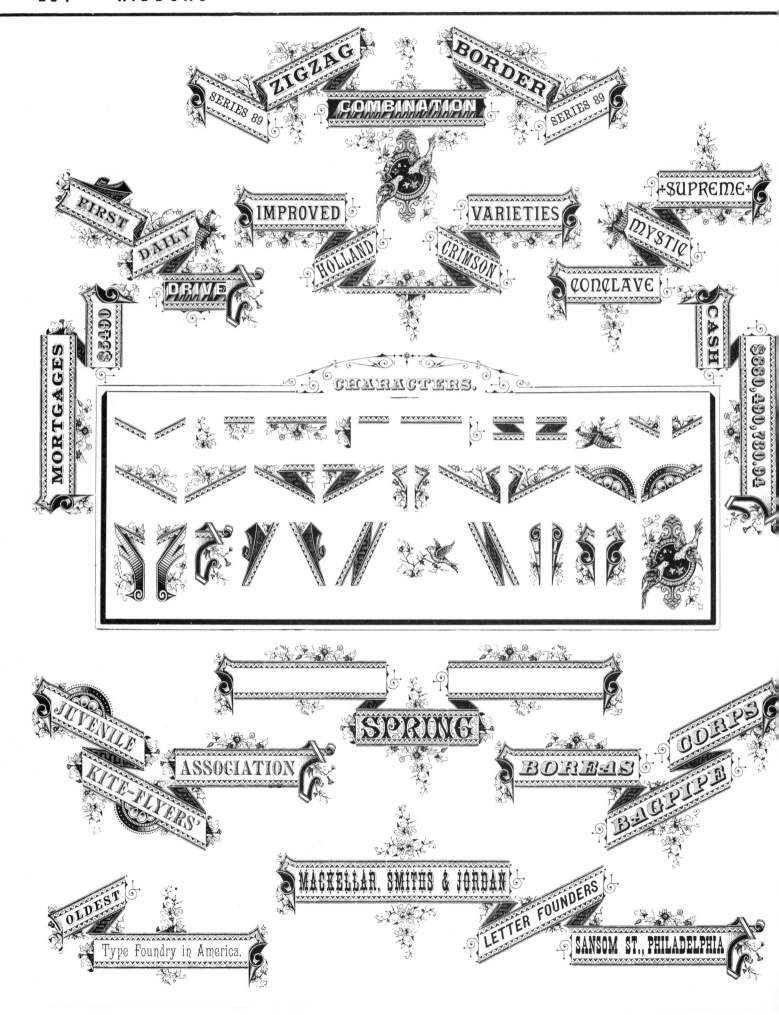

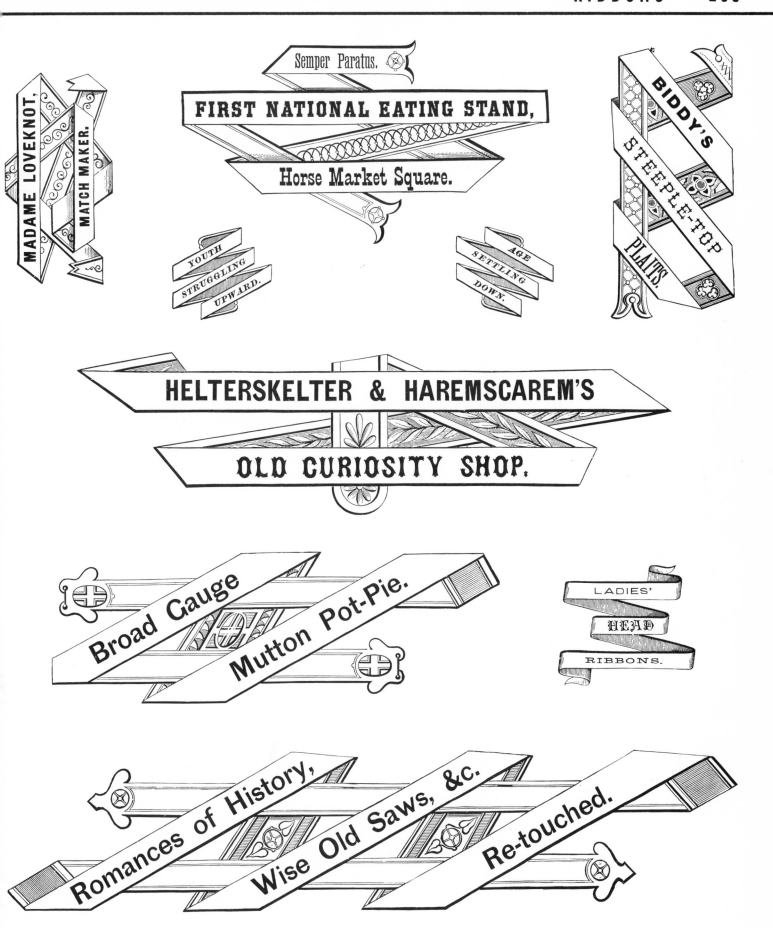

MADAME LOVEKNOT,

MATCH MAKER.

Semper Paratus.

FIRST NATIONAL EATING STAND,

Horse Market Square.

YOUTH STRUGGLING UPWARD.

AGE SETTLING DOWN.

BIDDY'S STEEPLE-TOP PLAITS.

HELTERSKELTER & HAREMSCAREM'S

OLD CURIOSITY SHOP.

Broad Gauge Mutton Pot-Pie.

LADIES' HEAD RIBBONS.

Romances of History, Wise Old Saws, &c. Re-touched.

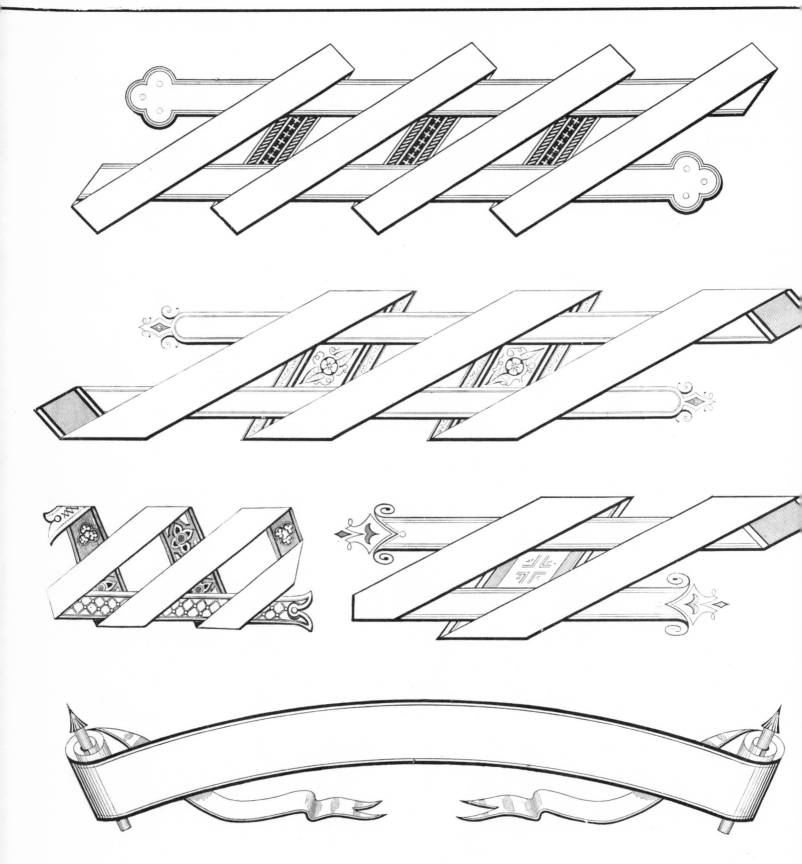

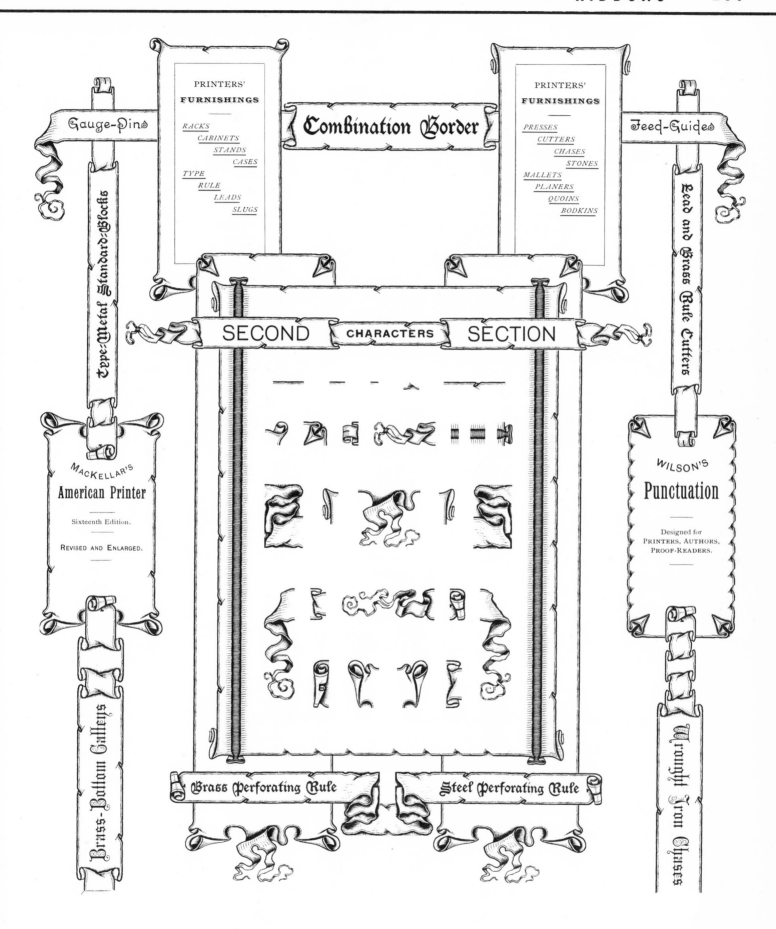

Gauge-Pins

Feed-Guides

PRINTERS'
FURNISHINGS

RACKS
CABINETS
STANDS
CASES

TYPE
RULE
LEADS
SLUGS

Combination Border

PRINTERS'
FURNISHINGS

PRESSES
CUTTERS
CHASES
STONES

MALLETS
PLANERS
QUOINS
BODKINS

Type-Metal Standard-Blocks

Lead and Brass Rule Cutters

SECOND CHARACTERS SECTION

MacKellar's
American Printer

Sixteenth Edition.

REVISED AND ENLARGED.

WILSON'S
Punctuation

Designed for
PRINTERS, AUTHORS,
PROOF-READERS.

Brass-Bottom Galleys

Wrought-Iron Chases

Brass Perforating Rule

Steel Perforating Rule

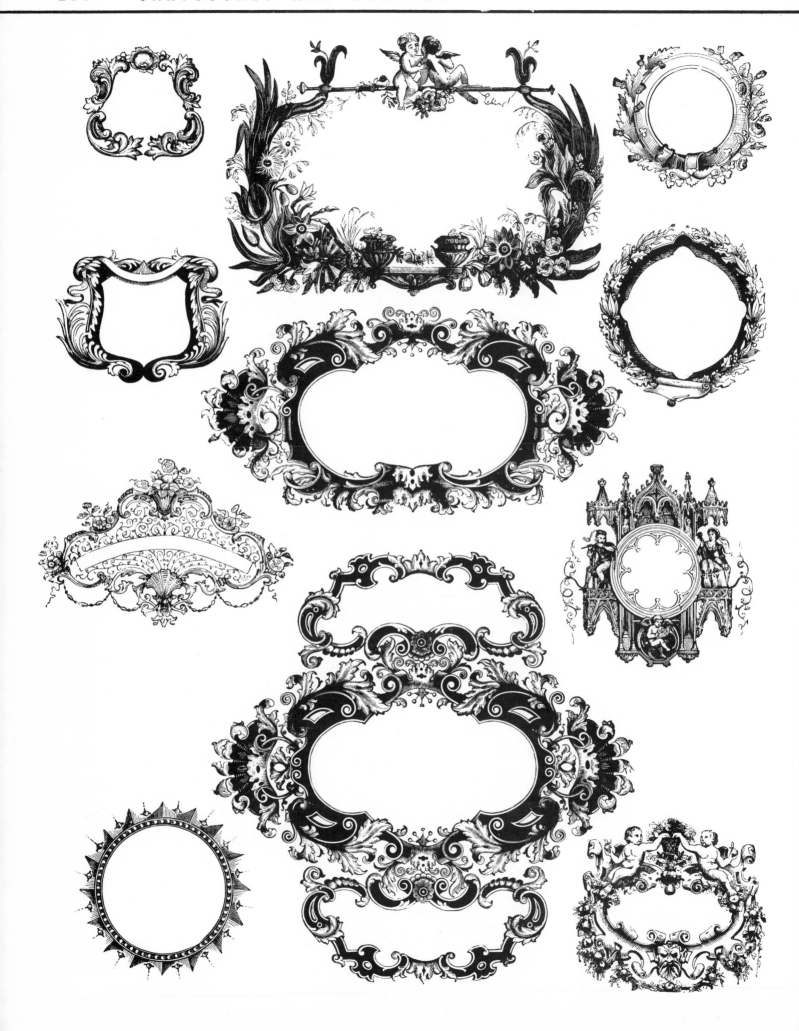

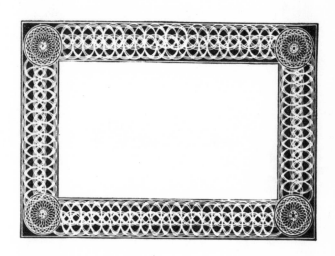

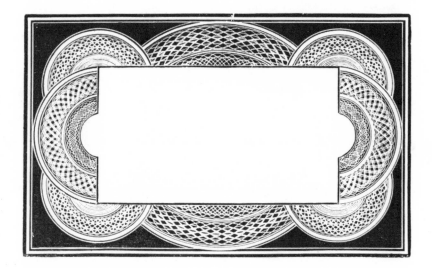

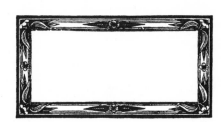

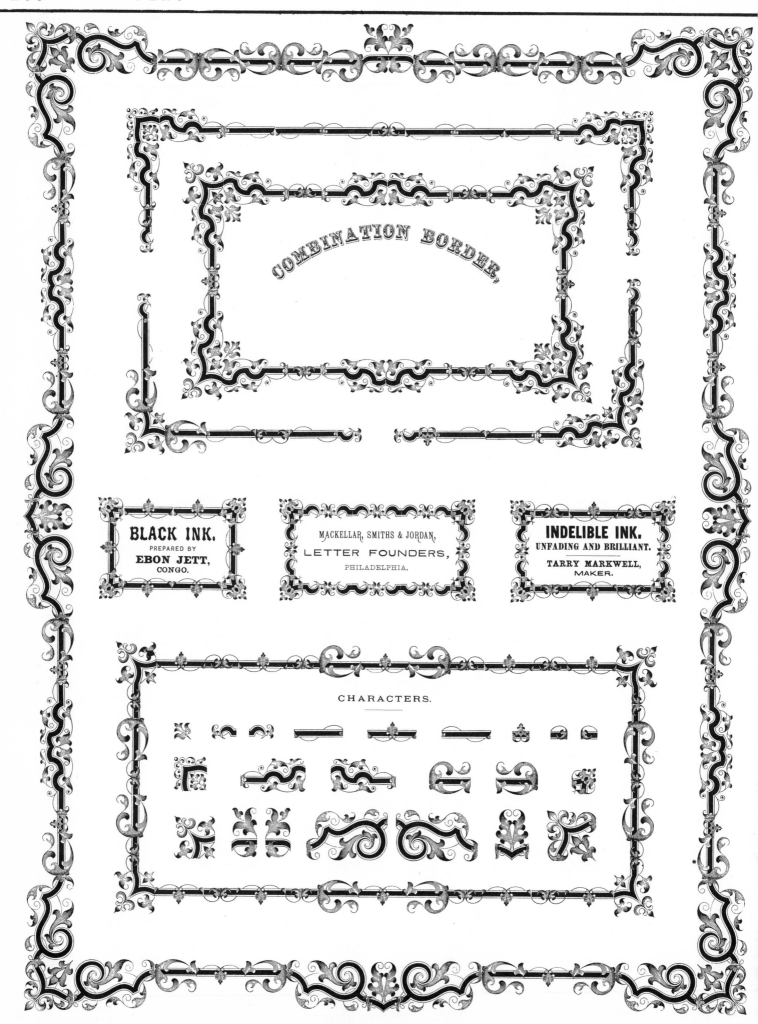

COMBINATION BORDER,

BLACK INK.
PREPARED BY
EBON JETT,
CONGO.

MACKELLAR, SMITHS & JORDAN,
LETTER FOUNDERS,
PHILADELPHIA.

INDELIBLE INK.
UNFADING AND BRILLIANT.
TARRY MARKWELL,
MAKER.

CHARACTERS.

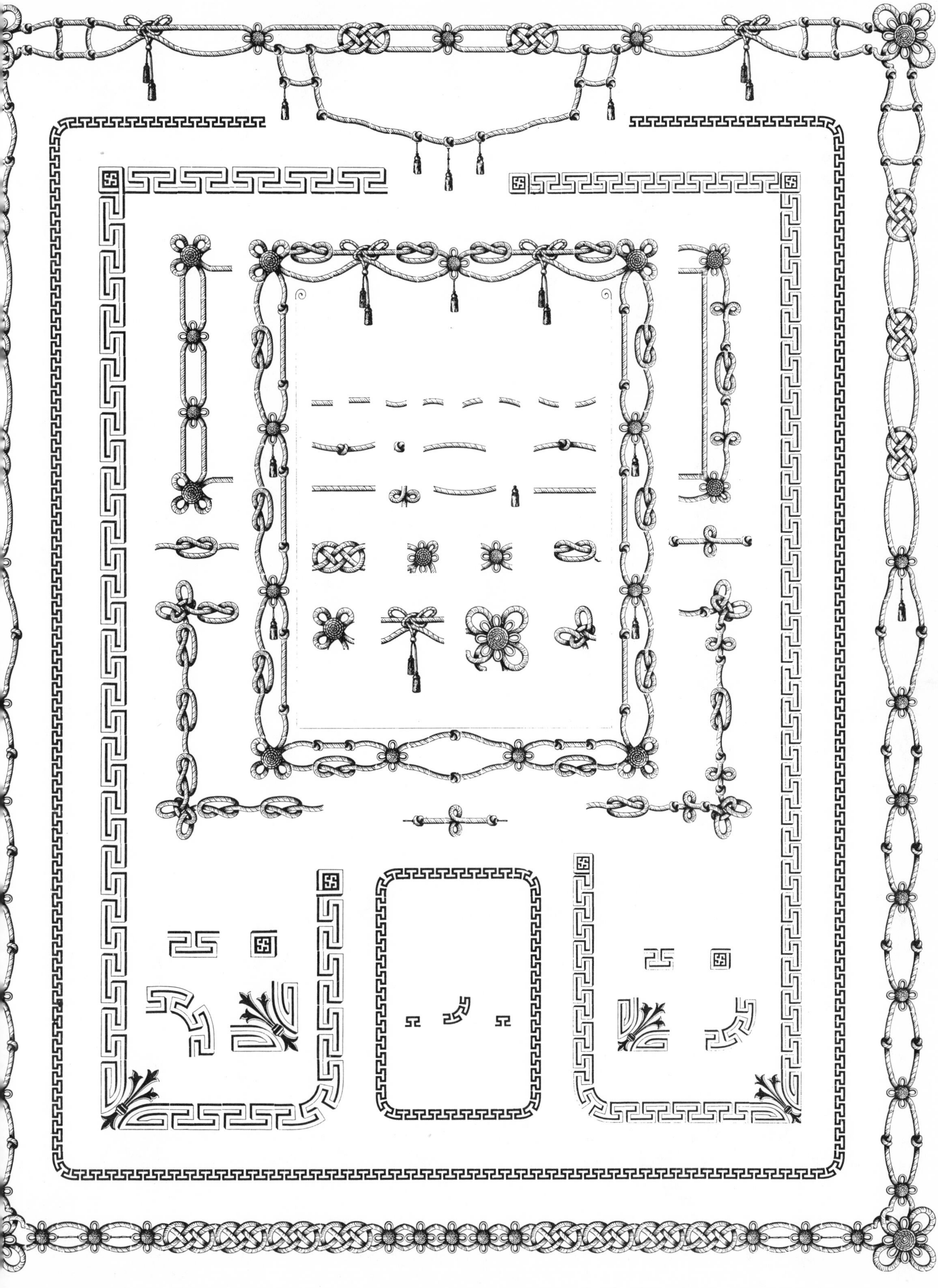

COMBINATION BORDERS.

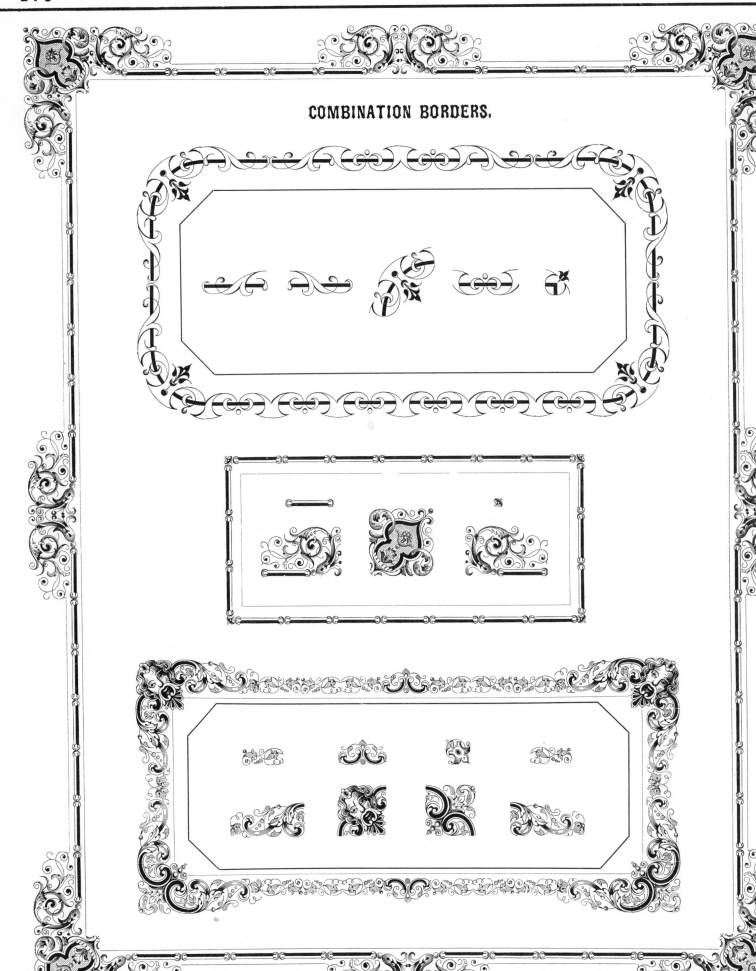

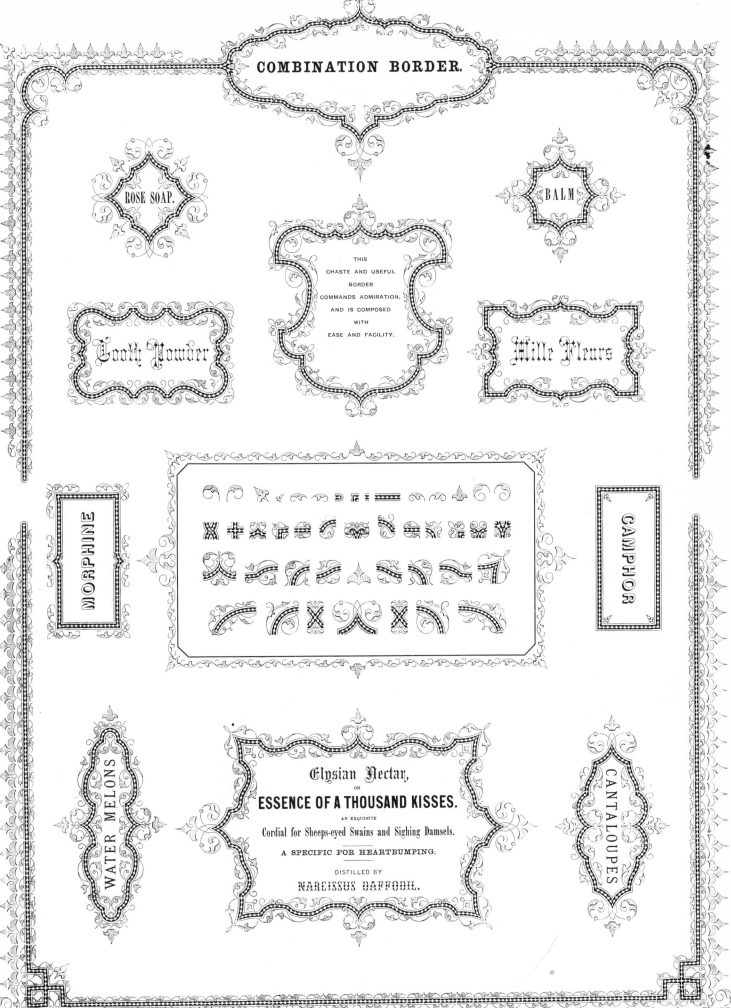

COMBINATION BORDER.

ROSE SOAP.

BALM

THIS CHASTE AND USEFUL BORDER COMMANDS ADMIRATION, AND IS COMPOSED WITH EASE AND FACILITY.

Tooth Powder

Mille Fleurs

MORPHINE

CAMPHOR

WATER MELONS

Elysian Nectar,
OR
ESSENCE OF A THOUSAND KISSES.
AN EXQUISITE
Cordial for Sheeps-eyed Swains and Sighing Damsels.
A SPECIFIC FOR HEARTBUMPING.
DISTILLED BY
NARCISSUS DAFFODIL.

CANTALOUPES

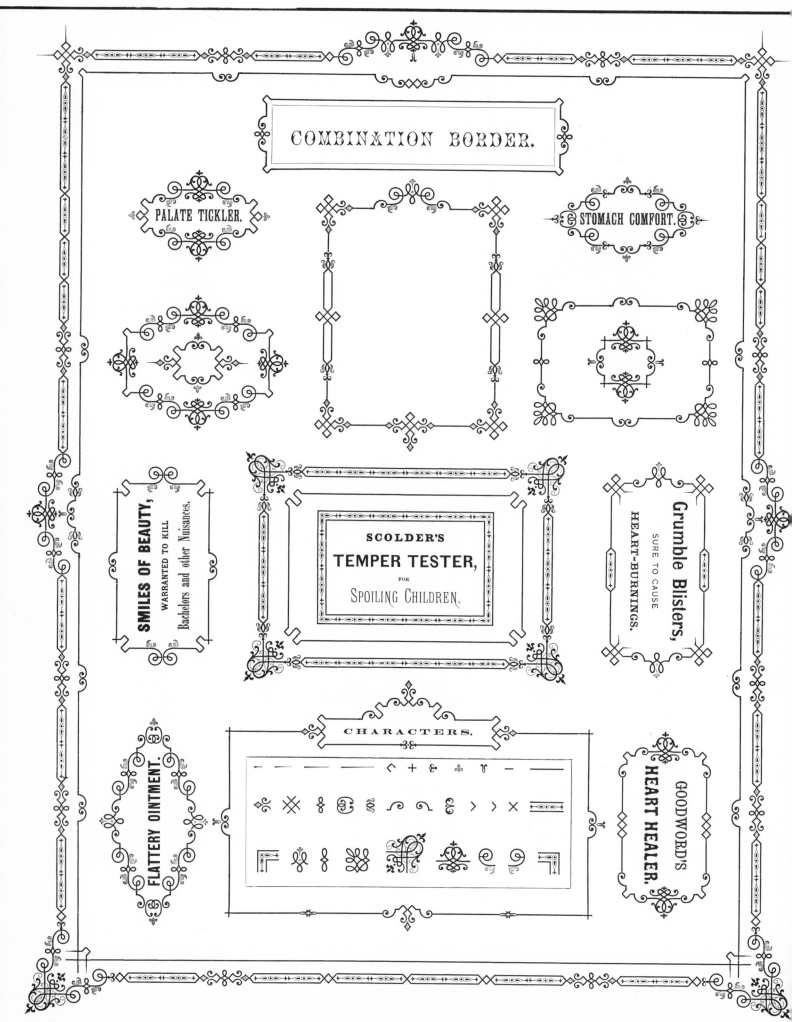

COMBINATION BORDER.

PALATE TICKLER.

STOMACH COMFORT.

SMILES OF BEAUTY,
WARRANTED TO KILL
Bachelors and other Nuisances.

SCOLDER'S
TEMPER TESTER,
FOR
Spoiling Children.

Grumble Blisters,
SURE TO CAUSE
HEART-BURNINGS.

CHARACTERS.

FLATTERY OINTMENT.

GOODWORD'S
HEART HEALER.

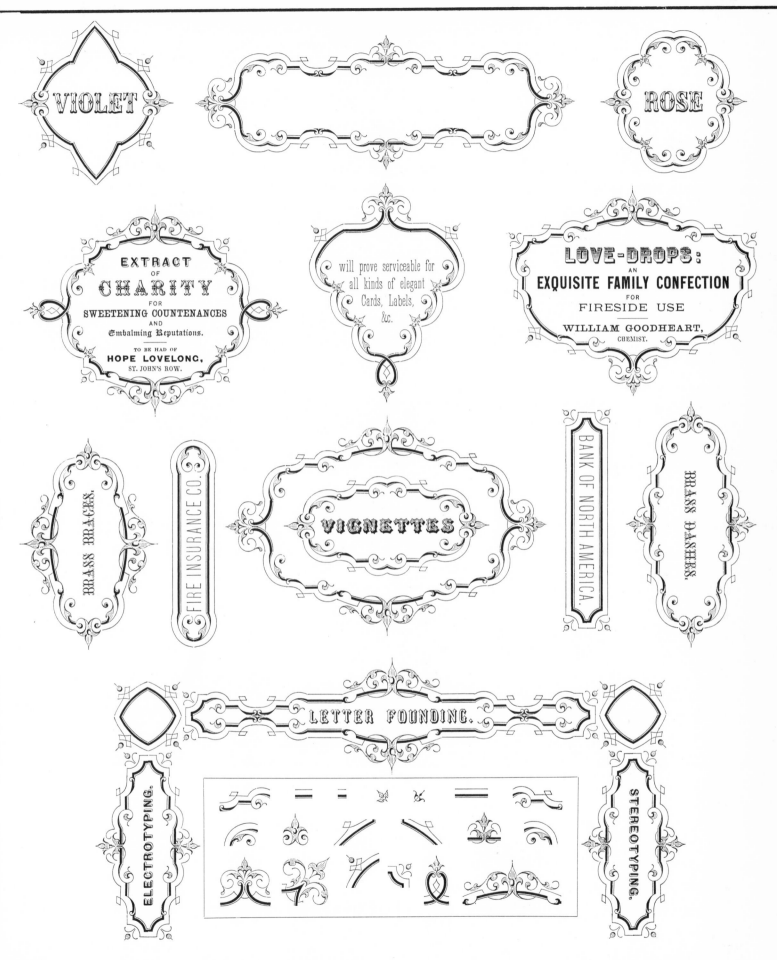

VIOLET

ROSE

EXTRACT
OF
CHARITY
FOR
SWEETENING COUNTENANCES
AND
Embalming Reputations.

TO BE HAD OF
HOPE LOVELONG,
ST. JOHN'S ROW.

will prove serviceable for
all kinds of elegant
Cards, Labels,
&c.

LOVE-DROPS:
AN
EXQUISITE FAMILY CONFECTION
FOR
FIRESIDE USE

WILLIAM GOODHEART,
CHEMIST.

BRASS BRACES.

FIRE INSURANCE CO.

VIGNETTES

BANK OF NORTH AMERICA.

BRASS DASHES.

LETTER FOUNDING.

ELECTROTYPING.

STEREOTYPING.

COMBINATION BORDER.

SIGNAL
LANTERNS
FOR THE
Prudent.

RED
LIGHTS
FOR THE
Reckless.

606-614

HOEDOWNS

A PERFECT CURE
FOR
THE BLUES.

STRAINS

FOR
TOOTHACHE
PAINS.

CHARACTERS.

VIOLET

EXTRACT
OF
RATAN
GOOD FOR
SAUCY CUBS
AND
Lazy Limbs

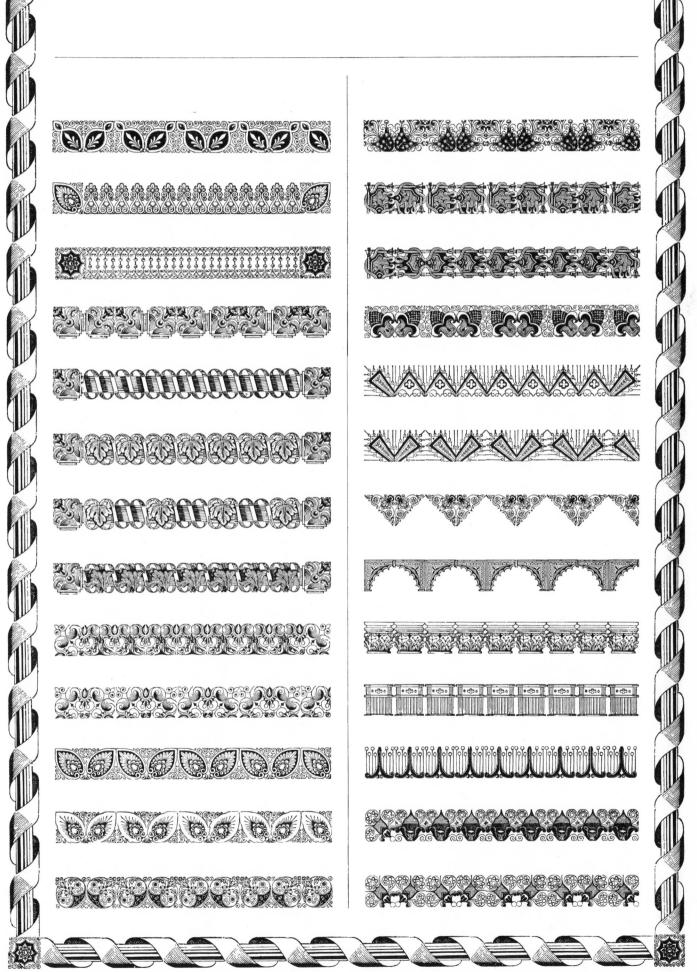

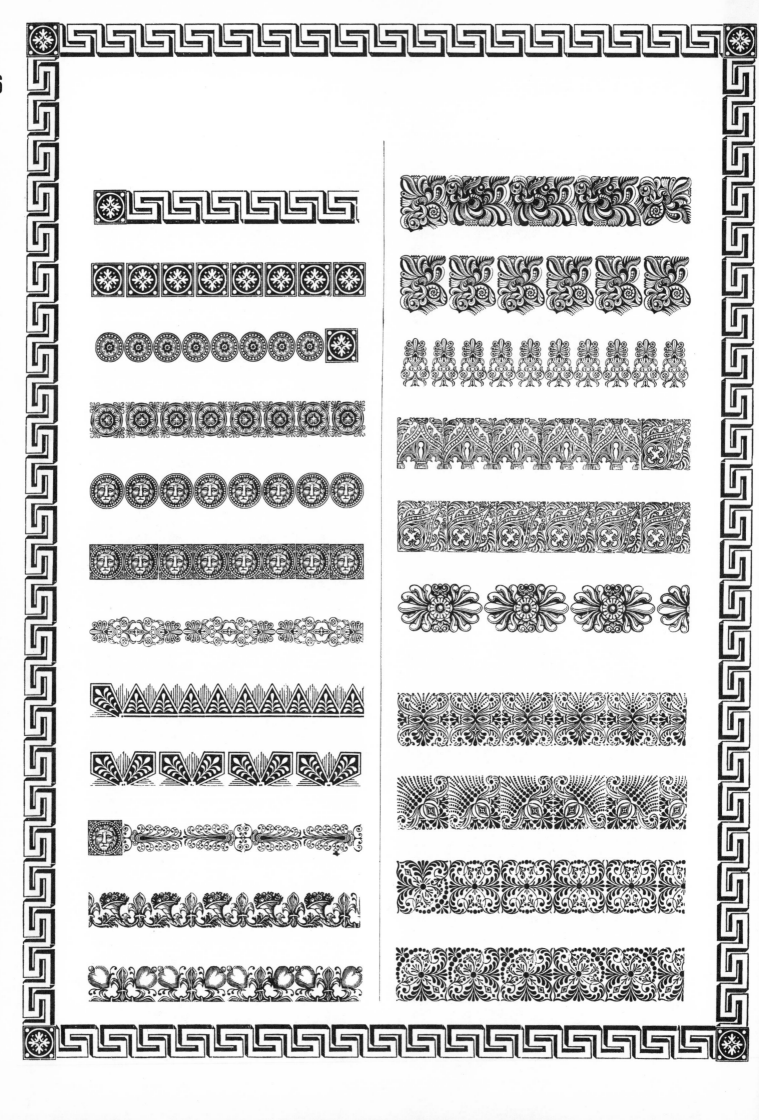

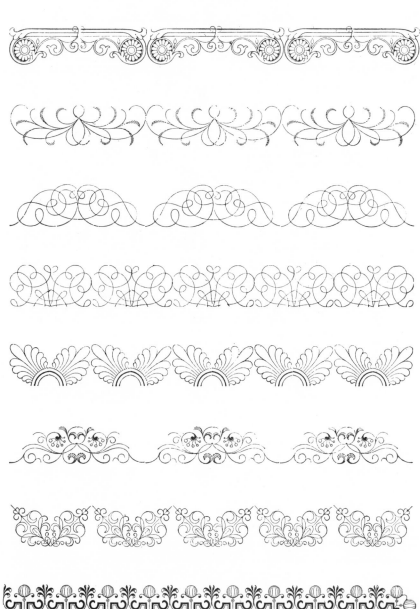

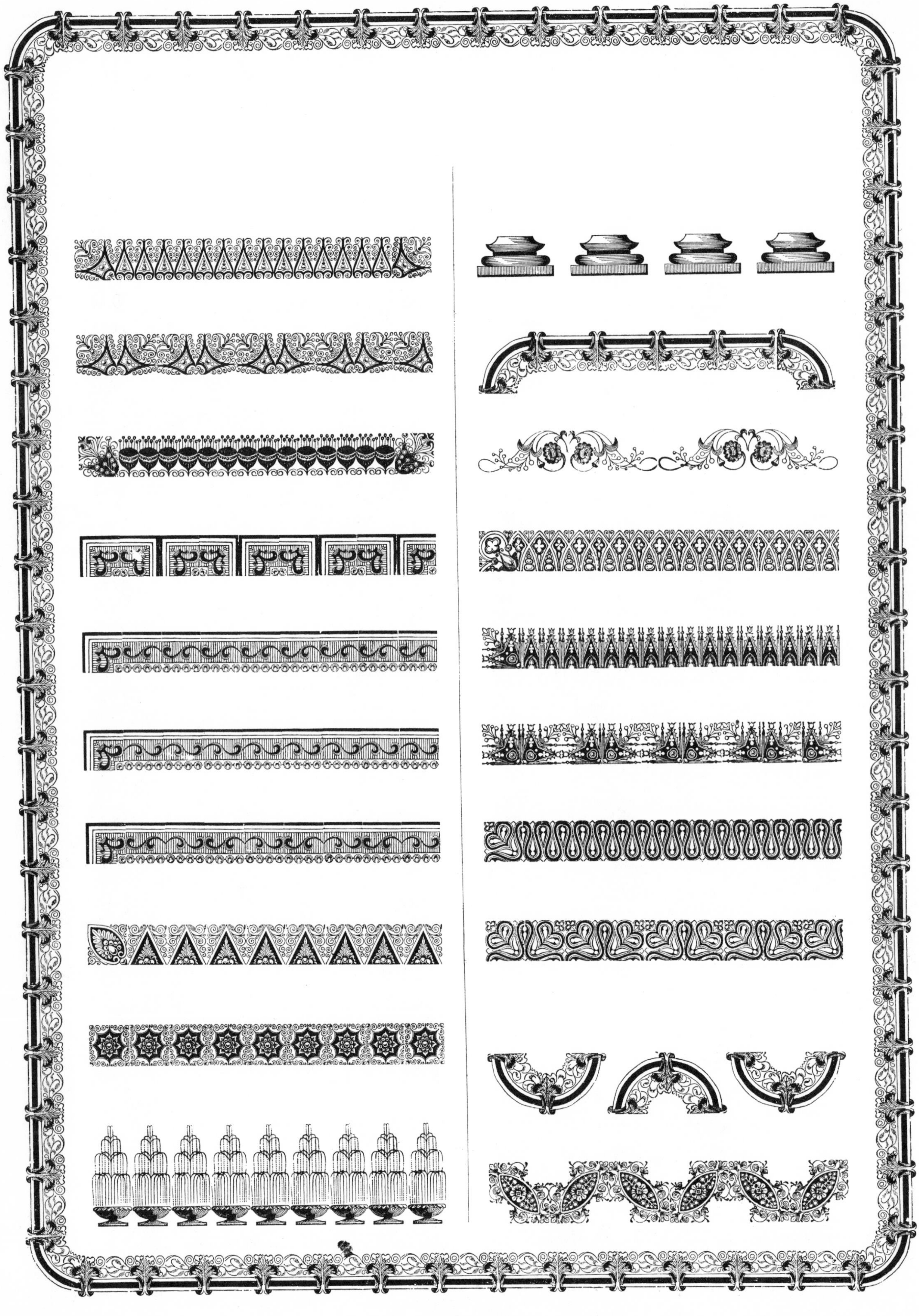

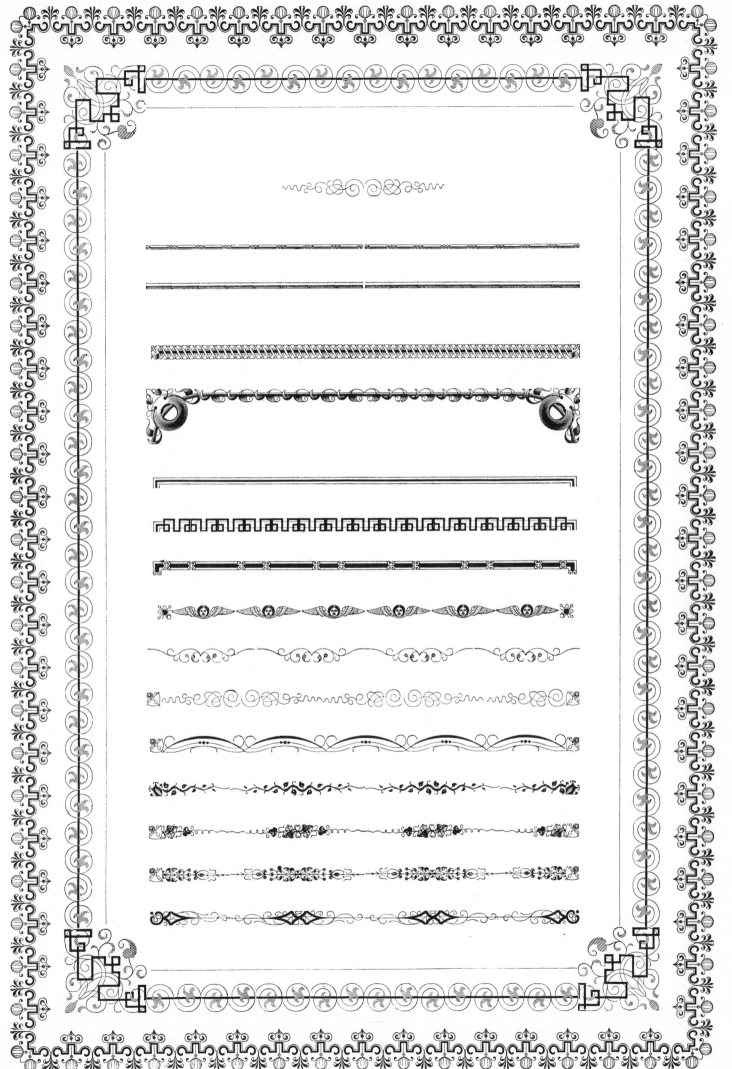

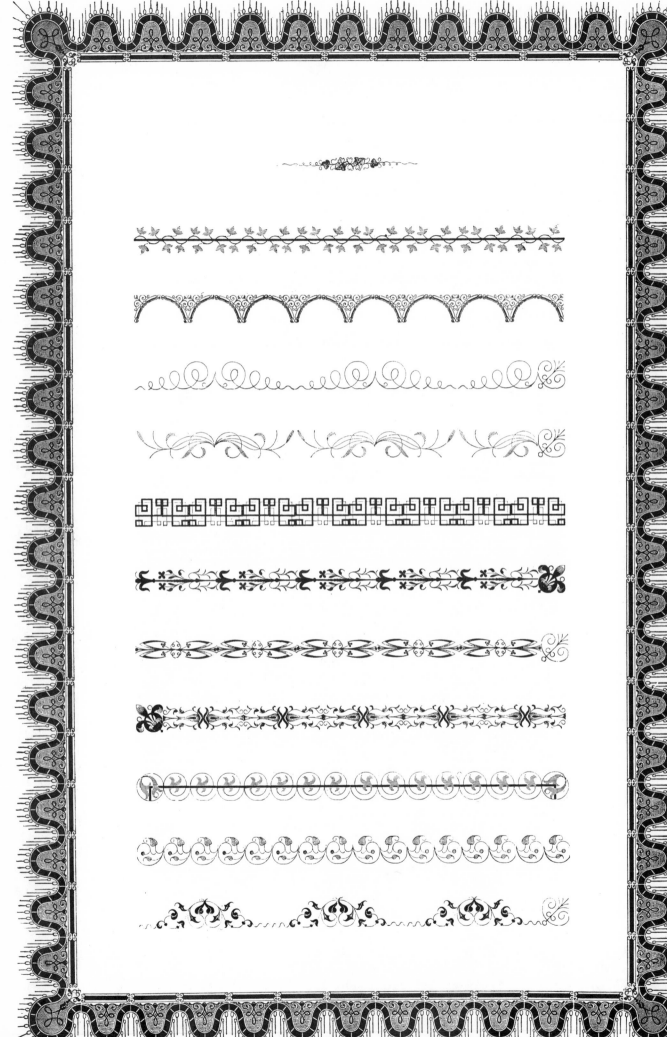

281

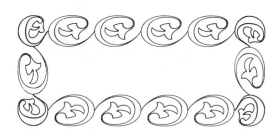

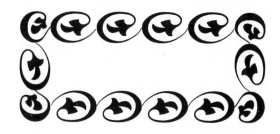

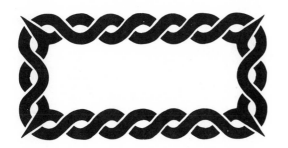

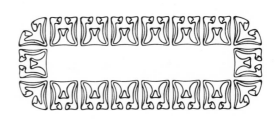

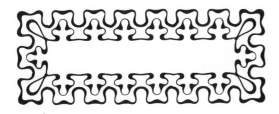

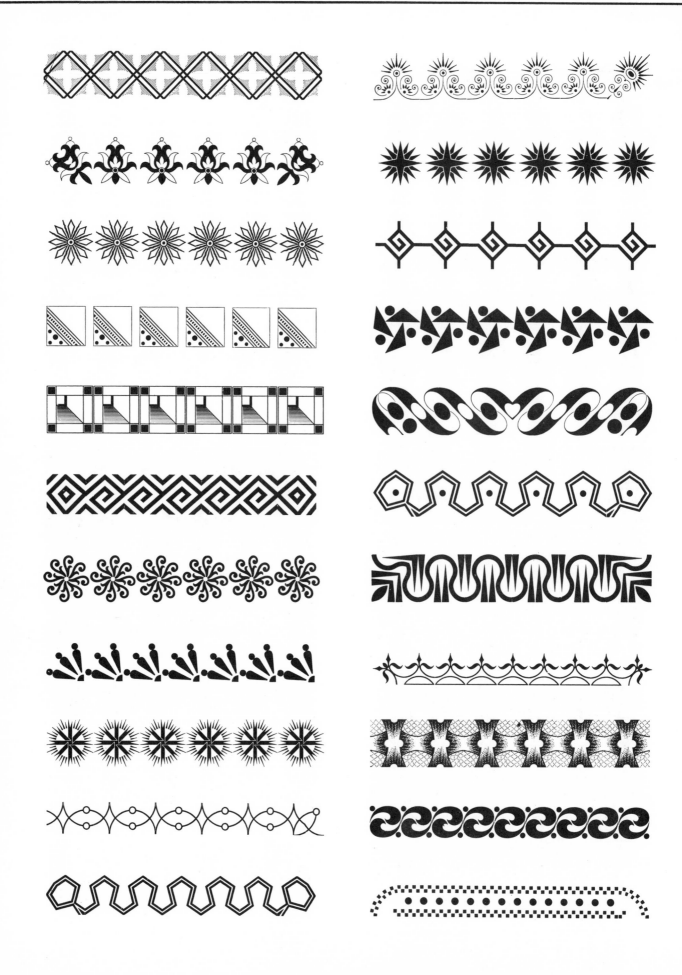

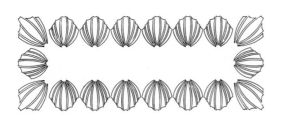

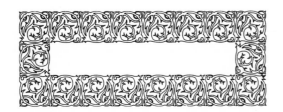

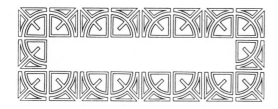

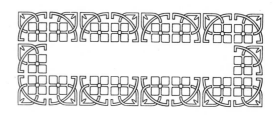

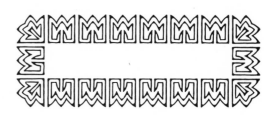

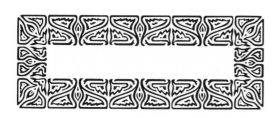

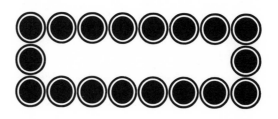

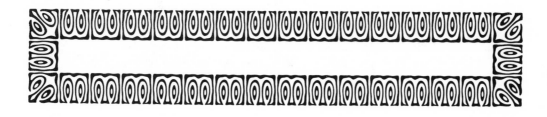

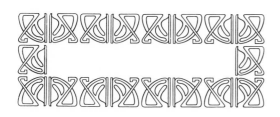

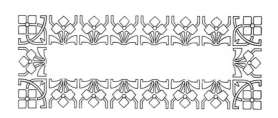

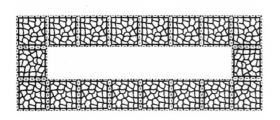

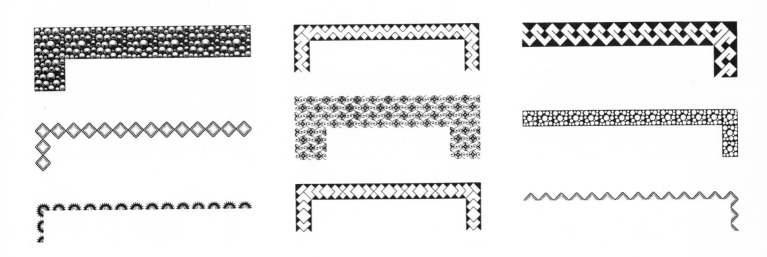

BORDER GEMS.

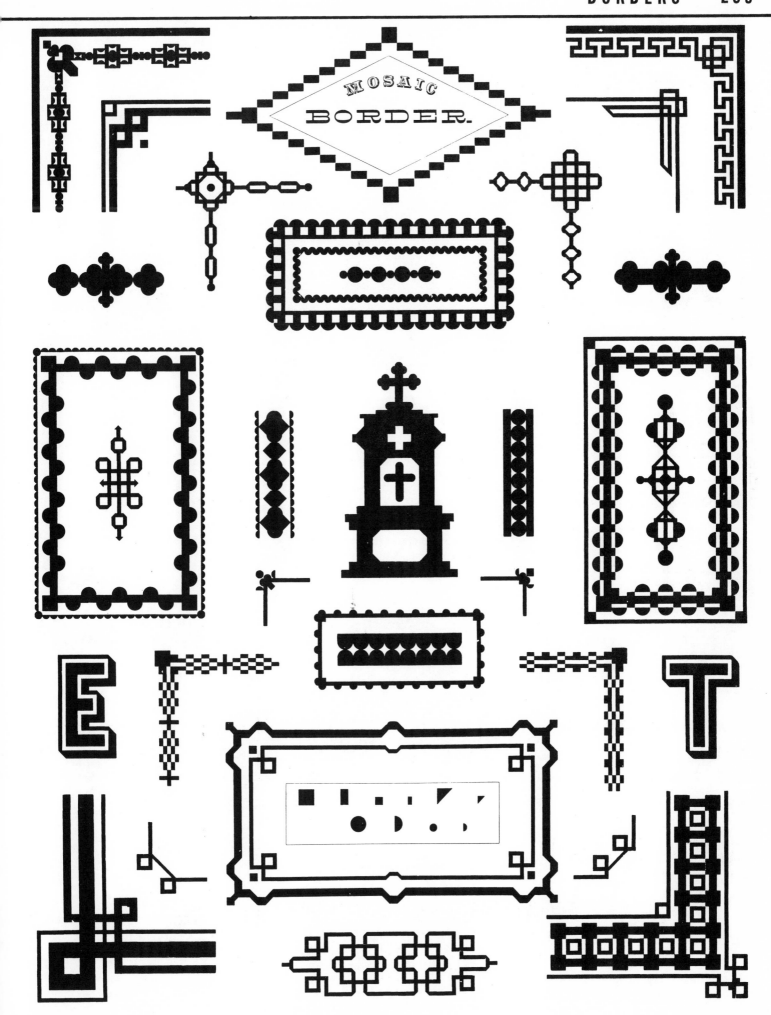

MOSAIC BORDER.

CHARACTERS.

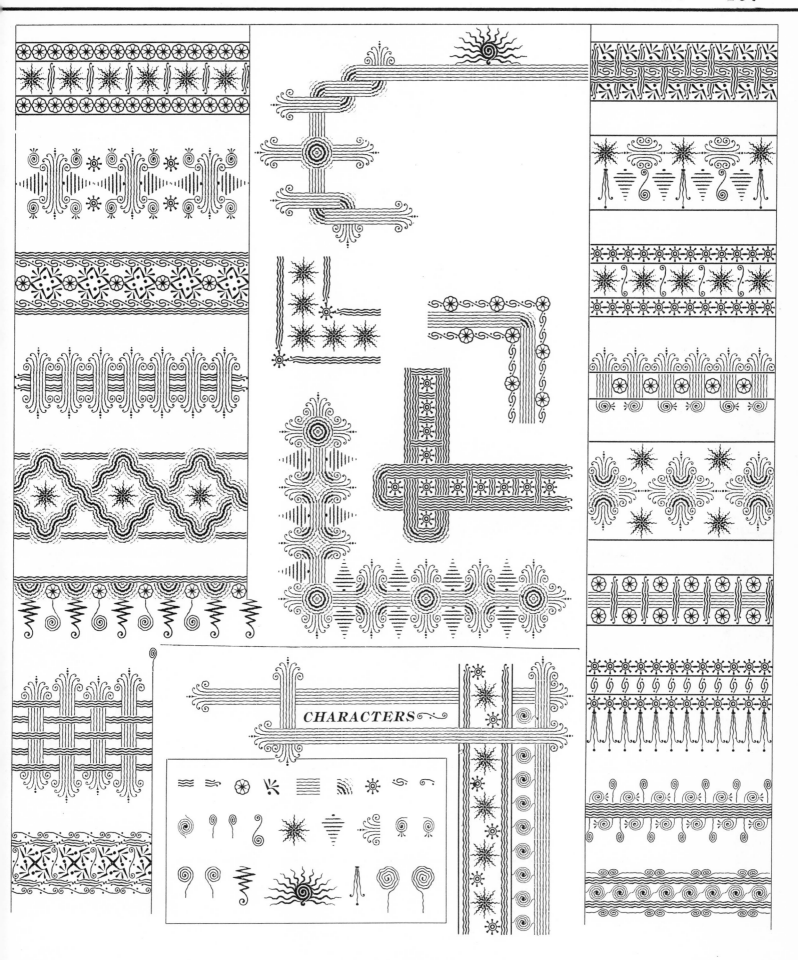

CHARACTERS

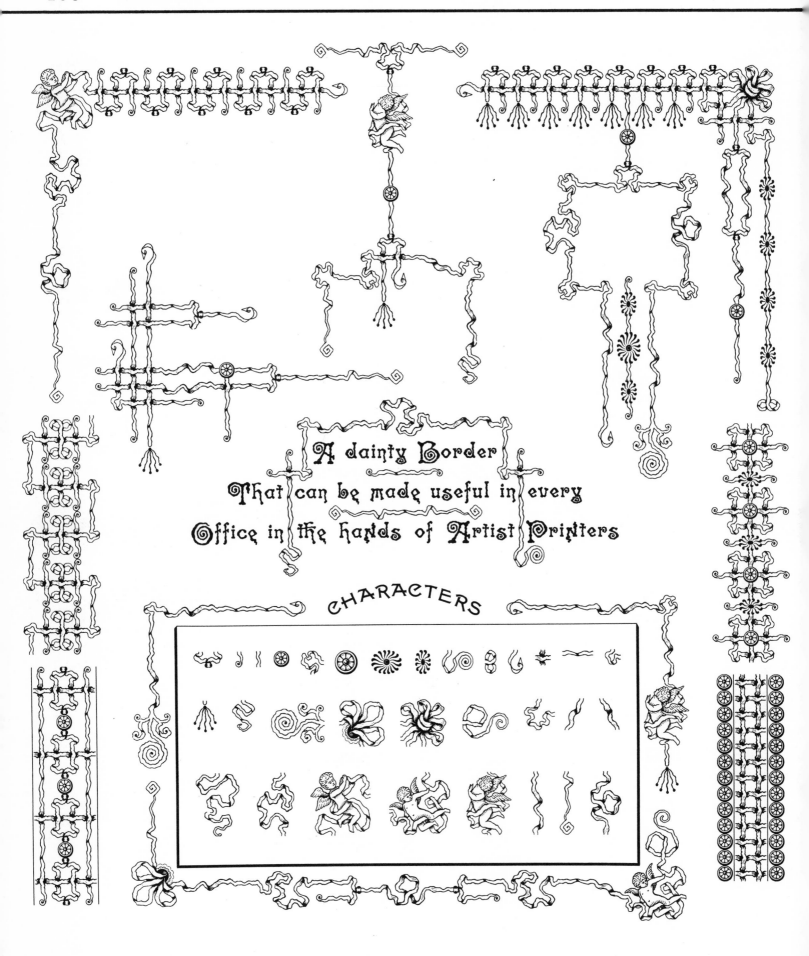

A dainty Border
That can be made useful in every
Office in the hands of Artist Printers

CHARACTERS

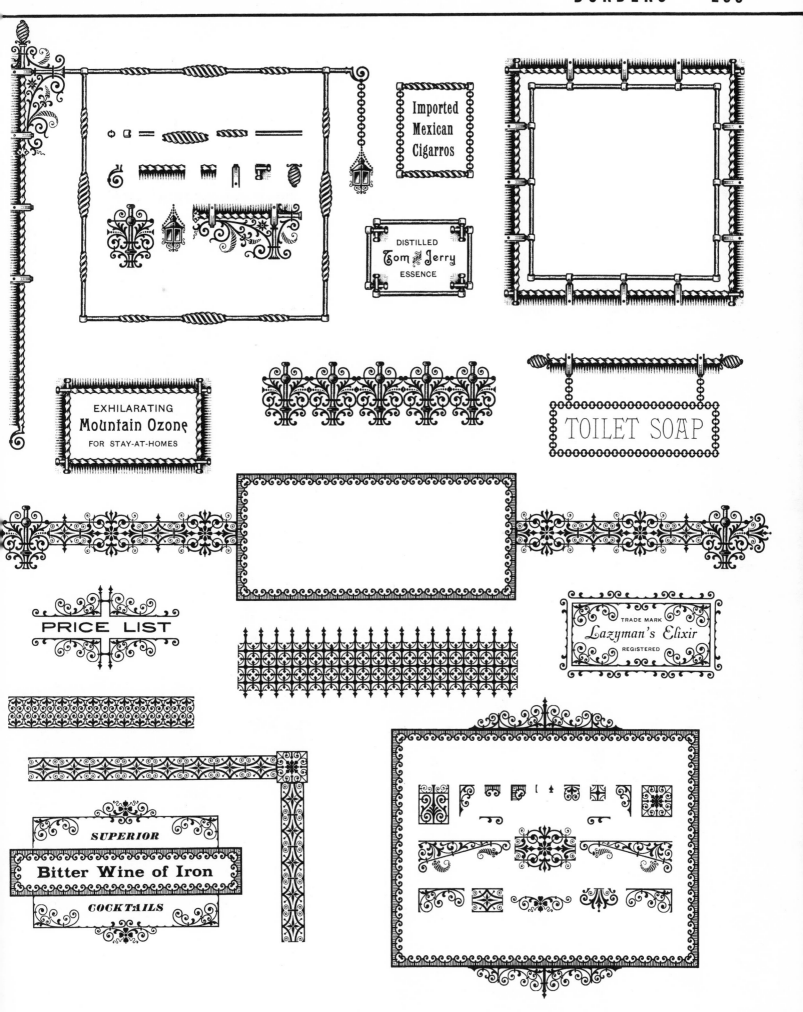

Imported
Mexican
Cigarros

DISTILLED
Tom and Jerry
ESSENCE

EXHILARATING
Mountain Ozone
FOR STAY-AT-HOMES

TOILET SOAP

PRICE LIST

TRADE MARK
Lazyman's Elixir
REGISTERED

SUPERIOR

Bitter Wine of Iron

COCKTAILS

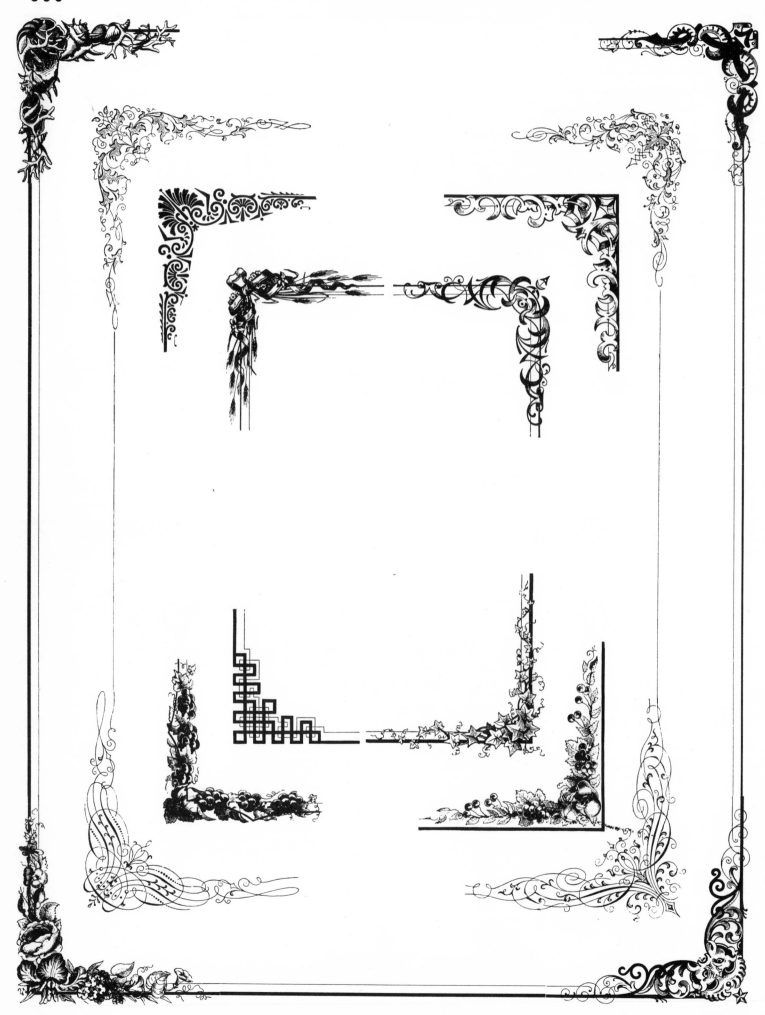

Temper Sauce.

COMBINATION
BORDER.

Slander Spice.

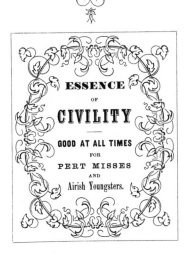

ESSENCE
OF
CIVILITY
GOOD AT ALL TIMES
FOR
PERT MISSES
AND
Airish Youngsters.

CHARACTERS.

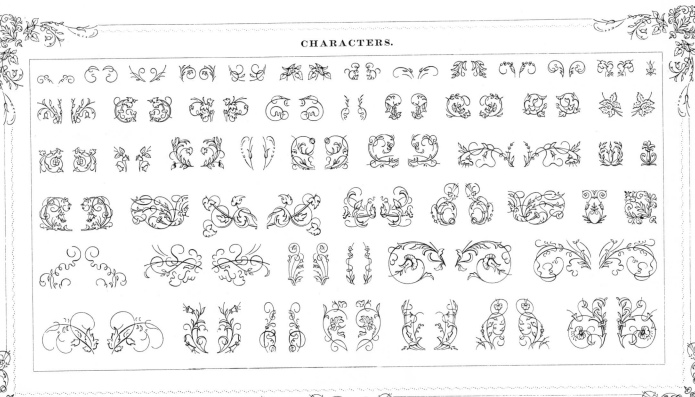

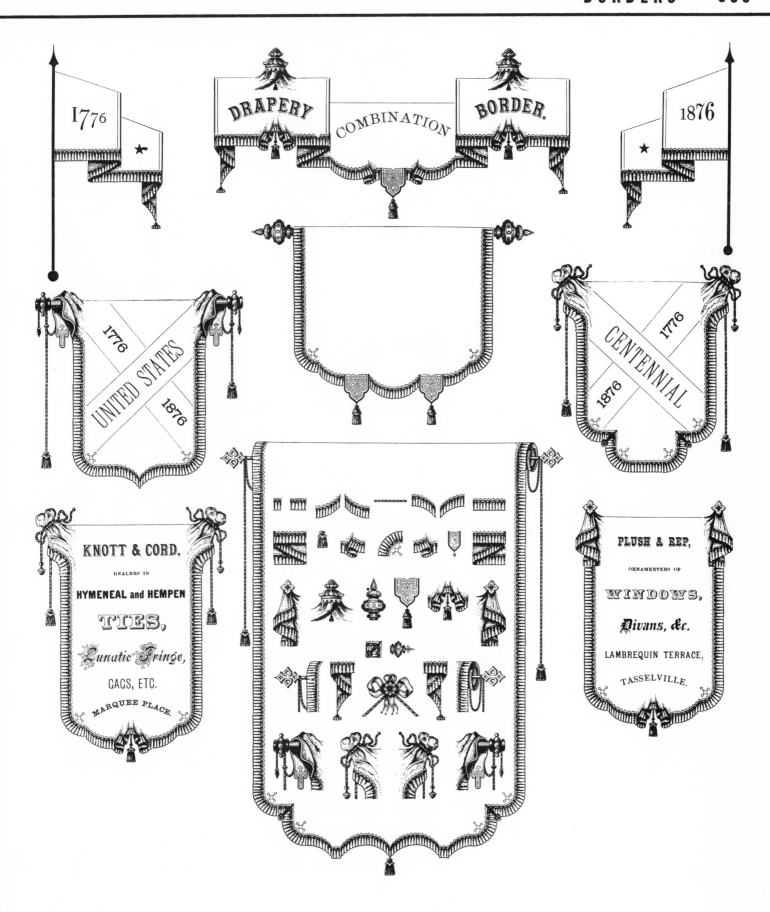

1776 1876

DRAPERY COMBINATION BORDER.

1776 UNITED STATES 1876

CENTENNIAL 1776 1876

KNOTT & CORD,

DEALERS IN

HYMENEAL and HEMPEN

TIES,

Lunatic Fringe,

GAGS, ETC.

MARQUEE PLACE.

PLUSH & REP,

ORNAMENTERS OF

WINDOWS,

Divans, &c.

LAMBREQUIN TERRACE,

TASSELVILLE.

OLD

RASPBERRY CORDIAL

1820

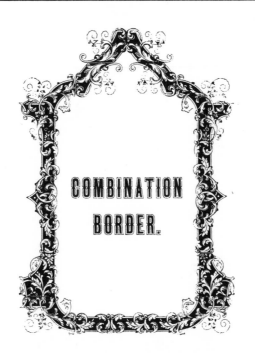

COMBINATION

BORDER.

RARE

CHERRY BRANDY

1796

PURE GRAPE

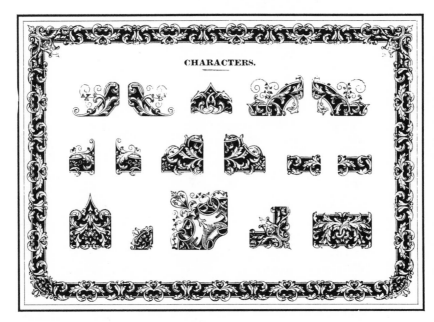

CHARACTERS.

SPARKLING CATAWBA.

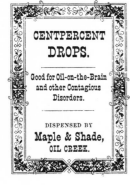

CENTPERCENT
DROPS.

Good for Oil-on-the-Brain
and other Contagious
Disorders.

DISPENSED BY
Maple & Shade,
OIL CREEK.

SERIES 66.

COMBINATION BORDER.

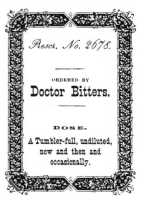

Prescr. No. 2678.

ORDERED BY
Doctor Bitters.

DOSE.

A Tumbler-full, undiluted,
now and then and
occasionally.

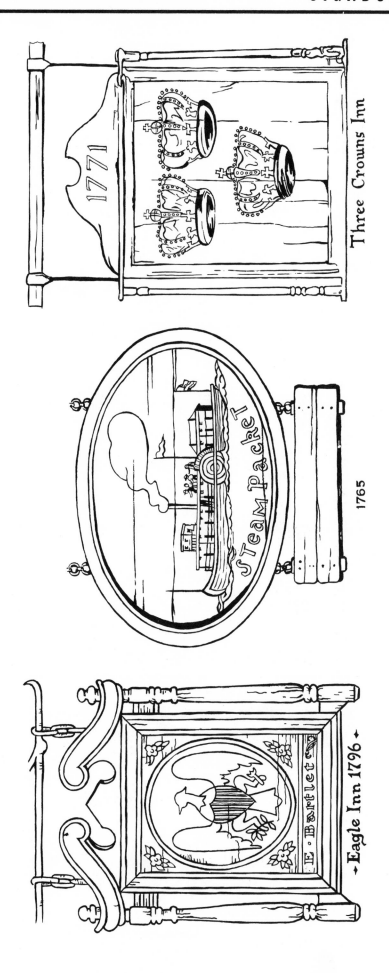

Three Crowns Inn

1765

Eagle Inn 1796

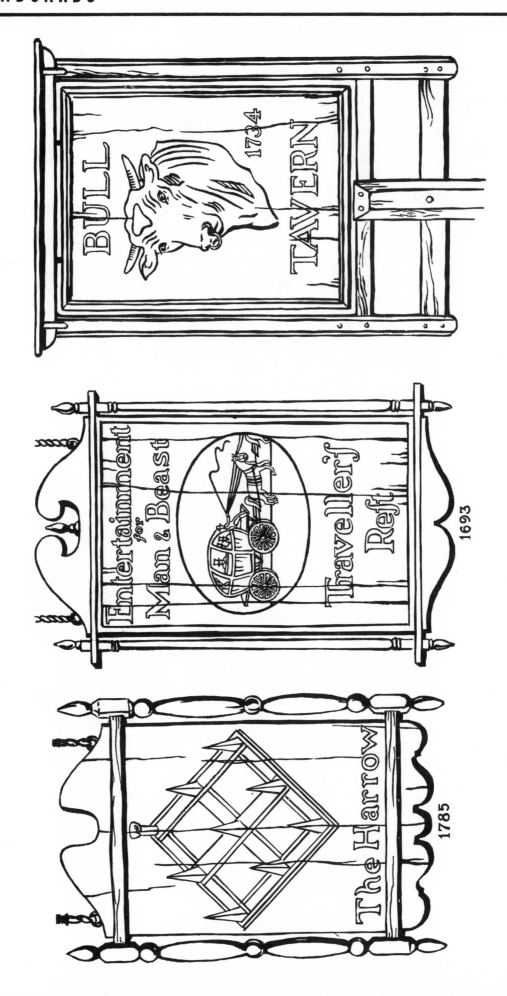

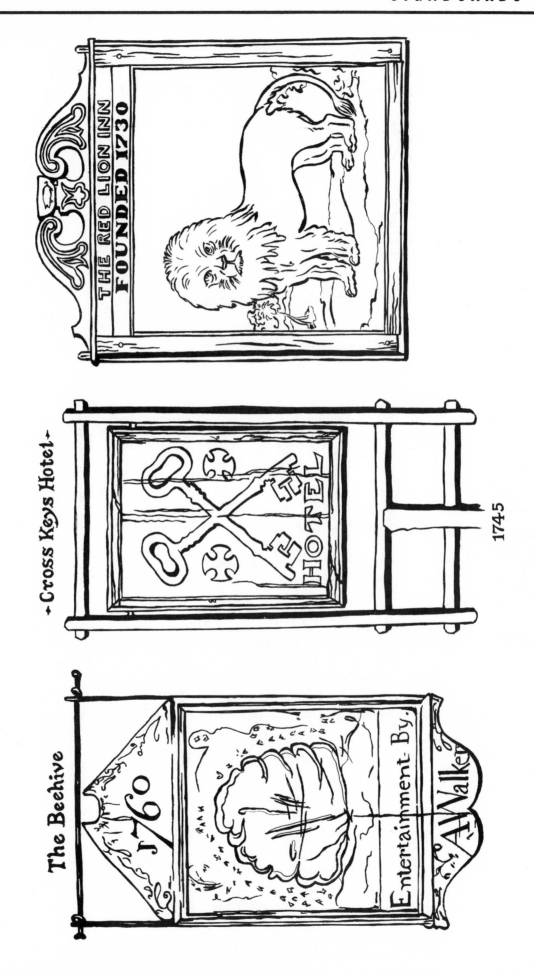

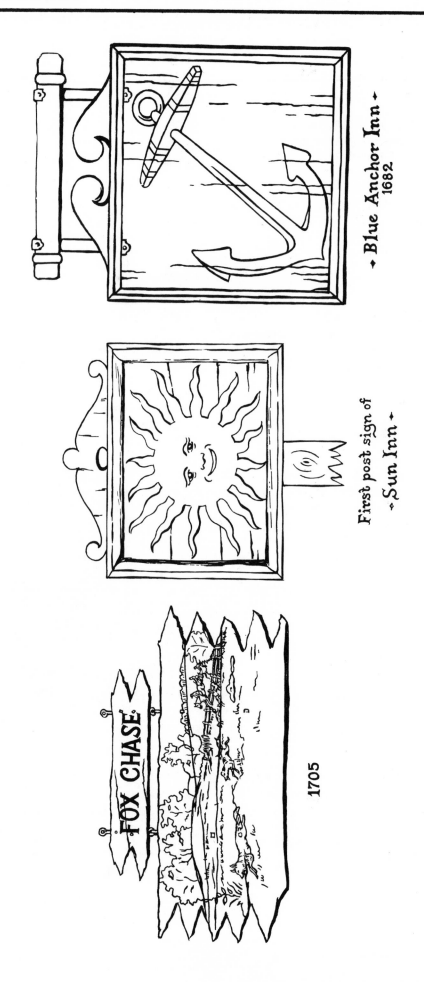

→ Blue Anchor Inn ←
1682

First post sign of
← Sun Inn →

FOX CHASE.

1705

The major sources of illustrations are type specimen books prior to 1890. Because the illustrations appear frequently in different catalogues and different years, the publisher believes that no useful or scholarly purpose is served by giving the exact source since no effort was made to reproduce or investigate their first appearance.

The following specimen catalogues were the main sources for this collection:

MacKellar, Smiths and Jordan.

White, John T. NEW YORK TYPE FOUNDRY SPECIMEN OF PRINTING TYPES CAST.

A. Zeese and Company.

James Conner's Sons.

Blomgren and Co.

Phelps Dalton and Co.

The following sources were also used:

Scrapbooks of the works of Dr. Alexander Anderson in the New York Public Library.

BALLOU'S PICTORIAL DRAWING-ROOM COMPANION.

HORSELESS AGE.

The Landauer Collection in the New York Historical Society.

THOMAS NAST'S CHRISTMAS DRAWINGS OF THE HUMAN RACE. Harper and Bros. 1890.

The material in the section of the Typographical and Ornamental Volume devoted to Alphabets and Decorative Initials was taken from the following books:

DECORATIVE INITIAL LETTERS, collected and arranged by A. F. Johnson:

Plates 165, 166, 168 to 170, 172 to 192, 214 to 216 (all inclusive)

SCHRIFTEN ATLAS, a collection made by Ludwig Petzendorfer, 1889:

Plates 194 to 197, 200 to 202, 206 to 210 (all inclusive)

EARLY WOODCUT INITIALS, selected and annotated by Oscar Jennings, M.D., in 1908:

Plates 167 and 171

SPECIMENS OF ELECTROTYPES, A. Zeese & Co., 1891:

Plates 193, 211 to 213 (inclusive)

PRANG'S STANDARD ALPHABETS, L. Prang & Co., 1878:

Plate 203

COPLEY'S PLAIN AND ORNAMENTAL STANDARD ALPHABETS, drawn and arranged by Frederick S. Copley, 1870:

Plates 198 and 199

OEUVRES DE JEAN MIDOLLE, published by Emile Simon Fils, Strasbourg, 1834-1835:

Plates 204 and 205

The plates of Trade Advertisements in the Pictorial Volume were taken from

AMERICAN PORTRAIT GALLERY, 1855

ILLUSTRATED AMERICAN ADVERTISER, 1856

The following check-list from the catalogue files of the Typographic Library of Columbia University, New York, represents the most complete collection of specimen books in America. The volumes were gathered by the late Henry Lewis Bullen, acting as curator and collector for the American Type Founders Company.

ALBANY TYPE FOUNDRY, R. Starr & Co., 1826.

BALTIMORE TYPE FOUNDRY, (Fielding Lucas, Jr., agent) 1832.
   "   "   " F. Lucas, 1851.
   "   "   " Lucas Brothers, 1854.
   "   "   " H. L. Pelouze & Son, 1879.

BINNEY & RONALDSON, Philadelphia, 1809.
   "   "   " 1812.

JAMES RONALDSON, Philadelphia, 1816
   "   "   " 1822.

BOSTON TYPE FOUNDRY, 1820.
   "   "   " 1825.
   "   "   " 1826, (John Rogers, agent)
   "   "   " 1828.
   "   "   " 1832.
   "   "   " 1837.
   "   "   " 1845.
   "   "   " John K. Rogers & Co., 1853.
   "   "   "   "   "   " 1856.
   "   "   "   "   "   " 1857.
   "   "   "   "   "   " 1860.
   "   "   "   "   "   " 1864.
   "   "   "   "   "   " 1867.
   "   "   "   "   "   " 1869.
   "   "   "   "   "   " 1871.

BOSTON TYPE FOUNDRY, John K. Rogers & Co., 1874.
   "   "   "   "   "   " c. 1875.
   "   "   "   "   "   " 1878.
   "   "   "   "   "   " 1880.
   "   "   "   "   "   " 1883.

BRUCE, DAVID & GEORGE, New York, 1815.
   "   "   "   "   " 1815-16.
   "   "   "   "   " 1818.

CHANDLER, A., New York, 1822.

CINCINNATI TYPE FOUNDRY, O. & H. Wells, 1827.
   "   "   "   "   " 1834.
   "   "   " (Horace Wells, agent) 1844.
   "   "   " (L. T. Wells, agent) 1851.
   "   "   "   " 1852.
   "   "   "   " c. 1853.
   "   "   "   " 1856.

CONNER & COOKE, New York, 1834.
   "   "   "   " 1836.
   "   "   "   " 1837.
   "   " (Supplement to the 1836 book)

JAMES CONNER & SON, New York, 1841.
   "   "   "   "   " 1850.
   "   "   "   "   " 1852.
   "   "   "   "   " before 1855.
   "   "   "   "   " 1855.
   "   "   "   "   " 1859.
   "   "   "   "   " 1860.

JAMES CONNER'S SONS, New York, 1870.
" " " " " 1876.
" " " " " 1885.
" " " " " 1888.
" " " .·. " " 1891.

DICKENSON TYPE FOUNDRY, (Samuel N. Dickenson) Boston, 1842.
" " " (Samuel N. Dickenson) Boston, 1847.
" " " (Phelps and Dalton) Boston, 1855.

FRANKLIN TYPE FOUNDRY, Allison, Smith & Johnson, Cincinnati, 1871.
" " " " 1873.

FRANKLIN LETTER-FOUNDRY, A. W. Kinsley & Company, Albany, 1829.

HAGAR, WILLIAM & CO., New York, 1826.
" " " " " 1831.
" " " " " 1841.
" " " " " 1850
" " " " " 1854.
" " " " " 1858.
" " " " " 1860.
" " " " " 1873.
" " " " " 1886.

JOHNSON & SMITH, Phila., 1834.
(Successors to Binney and Ronaldson
" " " 1841.
" " " 1843.

LAWRENCE JOHNSON, Philadelphia, 1844
" " " c. 1845.

LAWRENCE JOHNSON & CO., Phila., 1847.
" " " " 1849.
" " " " before 1853.
" " " " 1853.
" " " " 1856.
" " " " 1857.
" " " " 1859.
" " " " 1865.

MAC KELLAR, SMITHS & JORDAN, Phila., 1868.
" " " " 1869.
" " " " 1871.
" " " " 1873.
" " " " 1876.
" " " " 1877.
" " " " 1878.
" " " " 1881.
" " " " 1882.
" " " " 1884.
" " " " 1885.
" " " " 1886.
" " " " 1887.
" " " " 1888.
" " " " 1889.
" " " " 1890.
" " " " 1892.
" " " " 1894.

MAC KELLAR, SMITHS & JORDAN, Phila., 1895.
" " " " 1897.

LOTHIAN, GEORGE B., New York, 1841.

LYMAN, NATHAN & COMPANY, Buffalo, 1841.
" " " " 1853.

NEW ENGLAND TYPE FOUNDRY, Henry Willis, Boston, 1834.
" " " " George and J. Curtis, Boston, 1838.
" " " " " 1841.

OHIO TYPE FOUNDRY, Guilford & Jones, Cincinnati, 1851.

PELOUZE, LEWIS, Philadelphia, 1849.

PELOUZE, LEWIS & SON, Philadelphia, 1856.

REICH, STARR & COMPANY, Philadelphia, 1818.

ROBB & ECKLIN, Philadelphia, 1836.

ALEXANDER ROBB, Philadelphia, 1844.

STARR & LITTLE, Albany, 1828.

WHITE, ELIHU, New York, 1812.
" " " " 1817.
" " " " 1821.
" " " " 1826.
" " " " 1829.